ADHD

The Great Misdiagnosis

D0169778

ADHD

The Great Misdiagnosis

Revised Edition

JULIAN STUART HABER, M.D., FAAP

Taylor Trade Publishing
Lanham • New York • Oxford

First Taylor Trade Publishing edition 2003

This Taylor Trade Publishing paperback edition of *ADHD: The Great Misdiagnosis* is a revised edition. It is published by arrangement with the author.

Published by Taylor Trade Publishing
A Member of the Rowman and Littlefield Publishing Group
4501 Forbes Boulevard, Suite 200
Lanham, Maryland 20706

Distributed by National Book Network

Library of Congress Cataloging-in-Publication Data

Haber, Julian Stuart.
  ADHD : the great misdiagnosis / Julian Stuart Haber. — Rev. ed.
      p. cm.
Includes bibliographical references and index.
  ISBN 1-58979-047-2 (pbk. : alk. paper)
  1. Attention-deficit hyperactivity disorder—Diagnosis. 2.
Attention-deficit hyperactivity disorder—Treatment. 3.
Attention-deficit-disordered children. 4. Diagnostic errors. I. Title.

RJ506 .H9H334 2003
618 .92'8589—dc21

                                            2003007849

∞ ™ The paper used in this publication meets the minimum requirements of American National Standard for Information Services—Permanence of Paper for Printed Library Materials, ANSI/NISO Z39, 48–1992.
Manufactured in the United States of America.

To my wife, Marian, for her persistence, love, and encouragement, and in the memory of Warren Weinberg, M.D., professor of pediatrics and neurology and director of the Pediatric Behavioral Neurology Program, University of Texas Southwestern Medical Center at Dallas.

Contents

ADHD: The Great Misdiagnosis

Foreword

I remember the first time I met Julian Haber. It was thirty-one years ago! I had just earned my teaching degree and started teaching first grade at a private, college-preparatory school. That's when Dr. Haber, the pediatrician of one of my students, proceeded to tell me how I should teach the child in school. Because I clearly knew everything there was to know about instruction, I reacted by telling him something like, "I won't tell you how to practice medicine if you don't tell me how to teach."

I have since learned better. In the years since our first encounter, both of us have improved our learning. Julian has kept up with the latest research, particularly regarding students with learning difficulties. He has conducted scholarly research of his own. Besides maintaining his thriving pediatric practice, Julian has taught speech-language pathology students at Texas Christian University. My own realization of inadequacy, after a few years in the classroom, led me to earn a master's degree in special education with training as an educational diagnostician, special education teacher, and supervisor.

Foreword

Julian and I have crossed paths often over the years. We both have become advocates for children, particularly children with learning disabilities. Julian and I both served on the local council of the Learning Disabilities Association of America (which was called the Association for Children and Adults with Learning Disabilities). We were both charter members of the Special Education Advisory Committee for our school district. We have exchanged information with each other over the years as our interest and knowledge expanded.

Several years ago I asked Dr. Haber to speak to the faculty at an elementary school where I was the principal. Several teachers there fancied themselves as having medical knowledge. You know some of those teachers. They are the ones who tell parents, "Your child has attention deficit disorder. You need to take him to the doctor and get him some medicine." Julian, a developmental pediatrician, impressed the faculty with his knowledge and skills, but he impressed them even more because they understood what he was saying. He gave them information with a liberal dose of humor—information they could take into the classroom the very next day and use to improve the learning of their students.

Julian has written a book that I believe will be extremely helpful to parents and teachers. It is written to inform, but it is written in a way that is humorous and easy to read. I began reading the manuscript in a neurologist's waiting room. I became so absorbed in the text that I just sat there, laughing out loud occasionally, and forgot to worry about why I was there. Now that's engrossing!

Julian shares his expertise and experience in the book. He reports that, day after day, worried parents bring their children

Foreword

into doctors' offices because other adults have suggested that their children may have ADHD, or Attention Deficit Hyperactivity Disorder. All too frequently doctors do a cursory examination and prescribe medicine to control ADHD. In the United States, so many children have been labeled with ADHD and medicated that methylphenidate (Ritalin) has experienced a six-fold increase in manufacture since 1990 (more than 90 percent of methylphenidate manufactured is administered to children). Such figures, Dr. Haber writes, imply "that America has an epidemic rivaling any that has besieged our population in the past century."

Of course, as Dr. Haber notes, some children do have "disorders of inattention, increased activity, and impulsivity." A good clinician looks at these disorders, however, as symptoms of a problem that may be present in any number of neurobehavioral disorders. Dr. Haber points out that it is the differential diagnosis of these disorders that results in correct treatment and educational practices.

Dr. Haber describes many of the disorders that present some of the same symptoms as ADHD in terms that are meaningful to parents, teachers, and medical parishioners. He addresses not only the diagnosis, but also the treatments, medical and otherwise. Parents whose children are correctly prescribed medication can learn what to expect and when. Teachers who work with children in the classroom or on a daily basis can learn ways to maximize their instruction for children with learning problems. More importantly, however, Dr. Haber offers parents hope for the future. His closing statements reflect his compassion for all children with learning problems. He writes, "Trying harder, getting help early, family support, self-esteem, and acquiring alternative skills can help most children with differences to succeed." I cannot recommend Dr. Haber's commonsense approach too much. He provides a wealth of information and holds no cows sacred!

Margaret Carr
Executive Vice President,
Learning Disabilities Association of Texas;
former board member, Board of Directors,
Learning Disabilities Association of America;
member, Board of Directors, Advocacy Inc.

Preface

Recently, several authors have argued that Attention Deficit Hyperactivity Disorder (ADHD) is a myth. Nothing could be further from the truth. It is a very real entity has been called by many different names over the past fifty-five years. Perhaps as many as 15 percent of our children and adolescents are receiving medical treatment for ADHD, which can be severely devastating in the areas of learning, thinking, working, and social interaction. There is no question that the number of children diagnosed with the disorder is increasing.

On the other hand, the disorder is massively overdiagnosed, for a number of reasons. Are too many children being unnecessarily diagnosed and treated for the disorder? Or is the population with the disorder genuinely increasing? The answer to both questions is yes.

A number of other disorders, diseases, and problems display the same sets of symptoms as ADHD. Frequently, children with these symptoms are treated unnecessarily, or at times given medication for the wrong problem. This text addresses concerns

Preface

about inappropriate diagnosis and treatment that perplex many parents and professionals.

These problems are still present some three years and four printings after *ADHD: The Great Misdiagnosis* was initially published in August of 2000. Why then is it necessary to write a revision at this time?

There are now many new innovations and changes in the manner in which ADHD is treated and diagnosed. Some of the older treatment modalities have new dangerous side effects and problems not heretofore noticed. The present edition will extend to new areas not discussed at length in the first book. How can parents navigate the sometimes complex legal matrix in the school system to get help for a child with ADHD and other problems? What are some of the special problems encountered with teenage behavior? How does a parent help a young adult with ADHD move from childhood through junior high and high school, and then on to further education and various career options? How do parents select appropriate professionals to diagnose and treat their children? What are the coexisting conditions and how are they treated?

Unfortunately, many children are still being misdiagnosed. This is becoming increasingly recognized by national organizations such as the American Academy of Pediatrics, which recently issued appropriate guidelines for diagnosis and treatment. Now it is up to parents and professionals to understand these parameters and to make sure that no child is tagged with an inappropriate diagnosis and that all children are properly and comprehensively treated when appropriate.

This book is different from other ADHD books on the market because it addresses what Attention Deficit Hyperactivity Disor-

Preface

der is and what it is not. It exposes some of the chicanery that has led to an explosion of cases at epidemic proportions. Furthermore, it gives treatment options: medical, nontraditional, behavioral, and remedial. Finally, to make the text reader-friendly and understandable, I have illustrated complex concepts through the use of real events in people's lives.

I wish to acknowledge the help of Dena Francoli Hanson, Lynne Harman, and Karen Keller of the Edwin Schwartz Health Science Library at Cook Children's Medical Center, Fort Worth, Texas, for their help and support in retrieving many of the materials used in this book. In addition I am indebted to Kathy Edwards, M.Ed., director of educational services at the Fort Worth Child Study Center; Christina Norris, R.N., M.S.R.N., C.P.N.P., Fort Worth Child Study Center; Donald Bishop, J.D.; and the DFW Writers Workshop for review of material and technical assistance. Lastly, I wish to thank my wife, Marian, for her endless hours of reading the text, her editorial comments, and her persistent prodding to help this project to completion.

J. S. H.
Fort Worth, Texas
October 2003

Introduction

As indicated by statistics in the American Psychiatric Association's *Diagnostic and Statistical Manual of Mental Disorders*, fourth edition (*DSM*-IV), and by the American Academy of Pediatrics' definition of Attention Deficit Hyperactivity Disorder (ADHD), the incidence of ADHD in the United States has remained between 3 and 5 percent for several decades. This is what might be called a cocktail party statistic. It seems to have begun circulating in the 1940s, when Professor Jones asked Professor Smith, "How many children do you think have problems with attention span and hyperactivity?"

"Somewhere between 3 and 5 percent," Smith answered.

And so it went from cocktail party to cocktail party, from professional conference to professional conference. Consequently, by the latter part of the twentieth century, when *DSM*-IV was published, the reported incidence of ADHD had never been changed to reflect the greater number of children diagnosed with the disorder.

However, in many schools, 15 percent or more of the student population take various medications for this malady. One mother with a student matriculating at a school for gifted students re-cently said that an entire class in that school was on medication at the behest of a teacher who believed that her students were inat-tentive and could perform better on psychostimulant medication. Common psychostimulants are Ritalin (methylphenidate), Dexedrine (dextroamphetamine), and Adderall (multiple salts of amphetamines).

In the fifty-county area in which I practice developmental be-havioral pediatrics, until two years ago it was not unusual in some schools to see lines stretching down the hallway from the nurse's office, as children waited their turn to take Ritalin and related drugs. Since the advent of longer-acting stimulant medications the lines have decreased. Nonetheless, the number of children on medication continues to increase. In some communities, such as coastal Virginia and the Detroit area, the greatest increase is in the lower socioeconomic populations, where medication has become a replacement for adequate educational remediation and psycho-logical and family services. In other areas, such as metropolitan Chicago, the greatest amount of stimulant medication is pre-scribed in the most affluent neighborhoods. At the 2002 annual meeting of the Pediatric Academic Societies, Dr. Marsha Rappley reported that a large quantity of stimulant medication was being prescribed to Michigan children without a recorded diagnosis of Attention Deficit Hyperactivity Disorder.

Indeed, in several states in the South and Midwest the incidence of Ritalin and Adderall use in the student population is much greater than elsewhere in the country. A study at a large referral center for child behavior and development in St. Louis revealed that more than 30 percent of the children referred for Attention Deficit Hyperactivity Disorder did not meet the diagnostic criteria for the problem. Nonetheless, almost 20 percent of the noncriteria group were already under treatment with Ritalin or similar drugs. In other words, many children were being medicated for a condition they did not have. (See Appendix 1 of this book for the American Psychiatric Association's description of ADHD provided in the *Diagnostic and Statistical Manual* IV, as well as the definition given by the American Academy of Pediatrics in Appendix 2.)

The United States Drug Enforcement Agency production quotas for methylphenidate increased by more than 3,000 kilograms between 1990 and 1995. More than 90 percent of methylphenidate is produced and prescribed for children and adolescents with Attention Deficit Hyperactivity Disorder. This represents an almost sixfold increase in the manufacture of this drug and perhaps is an indicator of the marked increase in the diagnosis of ADHD. The drug manufacturer Shire Richwood Laboratories reported almost a doubling in the number of prescriptions for Adderall between the June quarter of 1996 and 1999. In North Carolina the number of Medicaid children on methylphenidate increased from slightly more than 4,000 (4.5 percent) to more than 20,000 (9.8 percent) in a six-year period.

According to a 2001 article in the American Academy of Pediatrics' journal *Pediatrics*, the use of stimulant medications in preschool children between two and four years of age has tripled. A set of guidelines issued the following year by the American Academy of Pediatrics (AAP) revealed that between 1990 and 2000 there was a sevenfold increase in the use of Ritalin and similar medications. Attention Deficit Hyperactivity Disorder had become the most prevalent neurobehavioral disorder in childhood, and one of the most common public health problems in children between six and twelve years old. Thirty to fifty percent of all visits to the offices of mental health professionals are now for the diagnosis and/or treatment of Attention Deficit Hyperactivity Disorder.

The fear of misdiagnosis and overuse of medication led the AAP to develop a tool kit for the diagnosis of ADHD. Dr. Carole Lannon, chair of the AAP Guideline Implementation Efforts Committee, recently asserted that only 25 percent of clinicians use appropriate criteria when making the diagnosis. "Sometimes doctors just sort of talk to people and put the child on a drug," she said in an interview. Five times as much medication is used in the United States as anywhere else in the world except Australia, which reported a threefold increase in the prescribing of stimulant medication between 1993 and 1996. If the manufacture and usage of medication and statements from professionals are indicators, then perhaps as much as 15 percent of our child and adolescent population is being treated or evaluated for Attention Deficit Hyperactivity Disorder. The implication is that America has an epidemic rivaling any that has besieged our population in the past century.

A few years ago, I appeared as a panelist on a nationally syndicated Public Broadcasting Service television show concerning Attention Deficit Hyperactivity Disorder. Five of us sat in front of the glaring white lights and cameras. Three panelists were professionals and experts in the field of child development, behavior, and education. Two others were parents of children diagnosed with ADHD. One panelist, a prominent accountant and partner in a large regional corporation, revealed that his son struggled in school and had problems with interpersonal relationships. The boy was eventually diagnosed with ADHD. With appropriate medical, behavioral, and educational management, the child had become quite successful. The father said that early identification and treatment of the problem had made a great difference in his child's life.

At the conclusion of the telecast, while chatting with this business executive, I learned that his son's psychiatrist also felt that the executive manifested symptoms of ADHD and started him on medication for the disorder.

"Aren't you an accountant and executive of a major corporation?" I asked.

"Yes, but when the psychiatrist began to ask me questions about my past, I realized that I, too, had the same problems as my son," he responded.

"Did you have problems in school, with relationships or friendships?" I further queried.

"No, I actually did well and had good grades in elementary school and all the way through high school. However, when I began college, I found that I was no longer the head of my class and it was a bit difficult for me to concentrate through my first two years," he recalled.

My curiosity got the best of me and I pursued the conversation. "From the introductions at the beginning of the program today I noticed that you graduated college, eventually got an M.B.A., and passed your public accountant certification examination."

"Yes, I did."

"Has your married and personal life been all right?"

Pulling out his wallet he displayed his portable family gallery. "Couldn't be better. My wife and I have been married for fourteen happy years, and we have two beautiful children. My boy has a few problems with ADHD, but we have that under good control. My daughter is an honors student and does quite well," the executive volunteered.

We shook hands, smiled amicably, and exchanged business cards. Here was a successful business and family man performing well within his environment. Yet a clinician diagnosed him as having a disorder.

Therein lies part of the problem with the current epidemic of Attention Deficit Hyperactivity Disorder in the United States. Do we really have an epidemic, or is an overzealous, entrepreneurial-minded group of people in the pharmaceutical, health care, and nonprescription drug industries promoting the disorder? Are well-intentioned periodicals presenting the public with partial and uncritical bits of information concerning ADHD that can be applied to many children who are normal?

If this is one side of the issue, then there are several other questions that need answering as well. Has the population of children, young adults, and adults with ADHD increased to a greater extent than knowledgeable professionals are willing to admit? Has there been an underdiagnosis of this disorder in the recent past, or has a large new population of young people with this problem suddenly arisen? Are professionals overdiagnosing the disorder by being intolerant of normal variations, or by using insufficient and inaccurate diagnostic criteria? Are parents, grandparents, and teachers intolerant of normal variants in motoric activity and inattention in children? Are experts in medicine, mental health, and education making the diagnosis of Attention Deficit Hyperactivity Disorder when other medical, sociological, or mental health problems are present instead? Lastly, is ADHD a relatively new disorder, appearing not long before it was first described in the third edition of the *Diagnostic and Statistical Manual of Mental Disorders* (*DSM*-III) in 1980?

ONE

What's a Parent to Do?

Parents can use many techniques to modify behavior of children with ADHD and to guide them. Some of these techniques are rule making, positive reinforcements, structured routines, information, color coding, limit setting, consequences, redirection, and posting reminders. Furthermore, parents need to approach any child with three key elements: patience, persistence, and consistency. These are even more important when dealing with a child diagnosed as having Attention Deficit Hyperactivity Disorder.

At age eight, Raymond Martinez could not stay on any schedule at home. Forgetting any series of tasks, he seldom completed anything. Much to his parents' frustration, Raymond's bedroom was a disaster. Clothes, bedding, and school supplies were tossed around everywhere. Homework time became a family feud. Assignments seldom made it home. When they did, the books Raymond needed to complete them frequently remained at school.

Mr. and Mrs. Martinez discussed the matter with Raymond's school counselor and his pediatrician. Obviously, the boy had great difficulty with self-regulation. Therefore, his parents set strict timelines for virtually every family function and routine.

For example, they began to eat at the same time every day. Raymond played at the same time every day, did his homework at the same time every day, and went to bed at the same time every night. Structuring in this manner helped build some semblance of a schedule. Eventually Raymond internalized this type of routine and compensated for his deficit in this area.

So that Raymond could concentrate on his homework, his parents placed him in a quiet work area with the fewest possible distractions. He was not allowed to study in his bedroom because it contained a bed, telephone, and television. They avoided the living room, which had an entertainment center and was heavily trafficked by other family members.

An adult in the household checked Raymond every few minutes to make sure he was on task. If necessary, the taskmaster used manual cues such as softly tapping Raymond's shoulder or gesturing, which reminded Raymond that he needed to continue his work. At fifteen- to twenty-minute intervals, Raymond was permitted to get up and walk around for five minutes, and then he returned to continue his school assignments.

The school counselor suggested that the Martinez family acquire a duplicate set of books from school to keep at home. Furthermore, his mother was to get his assignments for the entire week from his teachers, thus eliminating the excuse, "Mom, I forgot to bring my assignment home today," or, "Mom, I don't have any homework tonight, I think I'll go out and play."

Testing by a developmental pediatrician revealed that Raymond had problems with executive function and short-term memory. These problems impaired Raymond's ability to organize the surroundings at home and school. Schoolwork came home as backpack meltdown: papers and notes from several classes were mashed into one indistinguishable heap in the bottom of Raymond's backpack. His desks at school and at home were totally disorganized.

Raymond's organization and memory problems also affected his ability to follow a sequence of instructions. When Raymond's parents told him to go to his room, make up his bed, put his clothes away, and take out the trash, nothing got accomplished. Likewise, when his teacher gave several instructions at once, he seldom completed the assignment. She was lucky if Raymond completed the first two tasks out of a series of five or six instructions.

Children with sequencing, memory, or self-monitoring problems need brief instructions that are task specific. Mrs. Martinez began giving Raymond one or two instructions at a time. She would instruct Raymond to go to his room and make up his bed. After a couple of minutes, she would check on him and redirect him to his room if he lingered. Then she would tell him again to make up his bed. She might help him at first, then let him complete the task himself. Complimenting Raymond on a good job when he finished, Mrs. Martinez would next instruct him to pick up his clothes and to put his things away.

Another useful mechanism for helping young people with organization and memory problems is to post reminders. Pick out the two most important chores a day that you know your child can successfully complete. Then display a sign on the refrigerator and on a bulletin board in the child's room indicating the assignments for the day. Not only should the task be exhibited in writing, but an additional cue in the form of a picture should be placed next to the printed material. For example, "Make up your bed" may be accompanied by a picture of a bed and "Take out the garbage" by a picture of a trash can. After finishing the listed item, the child makes a check mark next to the completed task.

This technique is no different from adults using an organizer or similar written schedule to remind them of events in their lives that they might otherwise forget. Help your child to use this kind of system and to develop the habit of referring to such a source for information about daily activities.

Raymond Martinez's teacher suggested the method of color coding to help with his organizational skills. Raymond began using a different colored notebook for each subject: green for language arts, red for math, yellow for science, and blue for social studies. His teachers cooperated by making sure that, at the end of each period, the appropriate material was placed into the correct folder. They then had Raymond put the folder into his backpack. Now Raymond and his parents could find Raymond's school papers on the initial attempt. Each folder contained the papers appropriate for the proper subject, and made his life and homework considerably easier. Assignments from school weren't misplaced or lost. When homework was completed, Raymond's mother had him place the finished product into the specific colored folder for that subject.

Because Raymond's room and work areas were a disorganized mess, Raymond's father took the process one step further. If color coding helped at school, why not use it at home as well? Mr. Martinez created a red drawer for paper and school supplies, a green drawer for shirts and pants, and a purple drawer for underwear and socks, and so on. He found that when a small label was used to indicate color, it failed to achieve the desired result. However, when he covered the greater part of the drawer with the assigned color, accompanied with a printed label and a picture of the contents, the system worked quite well. In time Raymond's room became more organized and appeared less chaotic.

Ten-year-old Kelly Smith was a child in constant motion. Her impulsiveness manifested itself in riding her bike on busy streets, climbing trees, and jumping off her roof into the family pool. She frequently challenged bigger and older children to fights. Her parents feared for her safety.

Kelly's home behavior was equally dismal. Rarely did she follow her parent's instruction without a power struggle. She refused to follow family rules and routines. She became an expert at setting one family member against the other, knew what buttons to push, and constantly argued over any request.

Mr. and Mrs. Smith took Kelly to a developmental center where she was diagnosed as having Attention Deficit Hyperactivity Disorder, Predominantly Hyperactive-Impulsive. The center encouraged the family to follow several strategies. First and foremost, they instructed Kelly's parents to be consistent and to back each other up in front of the child. Once a rule was made, Kelly's parents were to enforce it and not allow Kelly to break the designated command.

However, if regulations are made every moment of the day for each minute behavior considered adverse, enforcement becomes meaningless and impossible. Children should be allowed to win on occasion on smaller issues. Therefore, Mr. and Mrs. Smith were told to make rules about the most important concepts. These included the rights of other people, personal safety, and essential chores.

Judgment must be used when determining rules for safety. For example, it might be all right to climb up to the first or second large branch of a tall tree, but certainly not to the top branches thirty feet off the ground. For a child with intermediate ability, swimming in a shallow pool with supervision would be permissible, but not going into a lake without supervision. Riding a bike on a quiet neighborhood street may cause no harm, but a child should avoid a busy thoroughfare. Certainly a child should always wear a helmet whenever riding a bike or rollerblading.

Considering the rights of others frequently involves a certain amount of good sense. Siblings usually battle for the same space and blame each other for disputes. Unless one of the children appears to be getting hurt, parents should try to stay out of these kinds of power struggles. For the most part, let the children settle the problem themselves. Many of us have the fantasy that no competition exists among brothers and sisters. Remember, they are fighting for the same space and for your attention. Fighting, feuding, and fussing in this arena is nothing new. The Bible is replete with tales about Cain and Abel, Jacob and Esau, and Joseph and his brothers—who did not sell Joseph into slavery because they loved him. Always try to be fair in these disputes; try not to take sides; intervene only if someone might be injured; do not give attention to just one child. Intervention may also be necessary if one child is much older or stronger than another.

Some examples of interfering with the rights of others are constantly interrupting family conversations, always having to have the last word, physically abusing other family members, not letting family members watch their own TV programs or talk on the phone, being argumentative, pushing, frequently calling names, destroying the possessions of others, and taking people's belongings without asking.

Important chore functions and rules may consist of taking out the garbage, doing the dishes, making the bed in the morning, going to bed at a set time each night without creating a fuss, helping clear the table, doing homework, coming to meals on time, and returning home when expected.

Rules must be simple, clear, and specific, and must have a time limit. Establish consequences for not following a rule. Offer a reward for proper performance and a penalty for not following a rule. When the penalty is taking something away, it must be something the child consider of value or enjoys. For example, parents may take away privileges such as playtime with friends, watching television, playing video games, or riding a bike.

For young adults, the ultimate objects and privileges that can be taken away are an allowance, the telephone, and the car. If all else fails, a threat to remove the child's privacy is useful. First the television and phone may be removed from a youngster's room, and then the door. No door, no privacy. Having no phone, no television, and no allowance makes life very boring for a teenager.

When using positive reinforcement for a child, do not give away the country farm. For younger children, offer things such as cards with pictures of cartoon characters, celebrities, or sports figures, or stickers. Older children or young adults may be given extra privileges, such as additional driving time, extended telephone use, or a small increase in allowance.

When Kelly insisted on riding her bike onto a busy thoroughfare near her house, her parents set a rule that clearly spelled out their expectations and had a penalty. "Kelly, you will not ride your bike onto James Street. If you do, you will lose the privilege of bike riding for the next two days."

ADHD: The Great Misdiagnosis

When you make a regulation, a child often will challenge it several times. In more difficult children this challenge occurs more frequently and repetitiously, particularly at the beginning. When parents are persistent and consistent, opposition to the rule becomes more intermittent. Eventually, the adverse behavior stops completely.

Kelly made several attempts to ride her bike on James Street. Each time, her parents chained up her bike for a couple of days. Eventually, Kelly got the message and the behavior ceased.

Try to change major problems one at a time. Do not attempt to accomplish several alterations in attitude at the same instant, since this can become confusing and accomplish little or nothing. In my private practice, I often ask parents to identify the most annoying or disruptive behavior their child exhibits. Frequently, I get a rather long list. I then ask for the two most difficult behaviors the parents are encountering. We discuss rule setting for each of these behavior problems, and the parents work on one consistently for several weeks before going on to the next.

Remember, it usually takes several years for a child to develop a certain behavioral style. Likewise, changes in these adverse attitudes may take days or weeks. Above all else, be persistent, consistent, authoritative, and calm. Never lose control or start a shouting match. If you have an adult temper tantrum, the child has won. Whenever you feel that you might lose control, walk away, take a deep breath, and reapproach the issue.

Eleven-year-old Keith Swenson frequently attempted to change the television channel when his family was watching a show selected by his parents. If his parents took away the remote, Keith walked back and forth in front of the television set whenever a program came on that he didn't like. Finally, his father established a rule. If Keith walked in front of the television to disrupt other people's enjoyment, he would be restricted to his room and lose all watching privileges for the next day. His parents would also remove the small television and telephone in Keith's room. When Keith broke the rule, his parents applied the penalty they had established.

"But that's not fair," Keith responded.

Mr. Swenson shrugged and replied, "Life's not fair, but the rule is that you will not walk continuously in front of us while we are watching a program. Because you did, you lost your watching privileges for today and tomorrow."

The boy frowned, stomped his feet, and screamed, "You don't love me. You hate me."

Mr. Swenson raised his eyebrows and waved his finger at Keith. "I love you, but I don't like your behavior. The rule is don't walk in front of people intentionally when they're watching a program. You did, so go to your room. No TV for today or tomorrow."

"I hate you! You always treat me this way," Keith shouted.

"You might hate me, but I love you and the rule still is that you will not intentionally walk back and forth in front of the family when we are trying to watch TV."

At a meeting of the Learning Disabilities Association of Texas in Austin, I passed by a conference room on my way to make a presentation. Hearing much laughter, I looked in. The speaker, Ed Gooze, a fellow presenter and consultant on communications and learning disabilities, was holding his audience spellbound. Ed was describing one of his methods for helping a child who engages in annoying behavior: point out the annoying behavior, and then state the expected behavior.

For example, if a child constantly interrupted you while you were talking on the telephone or with other people, you would say, "That's interrupting. Now let's practice waiting," without becoming angry and without otherwise responding to the child. Use a firm voice without anger. When the child waits for a few seconds or minutes, you may respond by saying, "That's very good. Now you are practicing waiting." After the positive behavior is well established, it is good to continuously tell the child that you are pleased by his correct choice of waiting. After a few times, offer to treat him to an ice-cream cone or a milkshake. When he asks why, respond, "Because you've done such a good job practicing waiting."

I have tried this technique with children at my office, as have several of the children's parents at home. The method really works quite well.

Another behavioral problem parents encounter is constant arguing. When you deal with an argumentative boy or girl, the key is to never argue. If you give an instruction as part of a rule and the child begins to argue, it is imperative to first say there are no arguments and then restate the rule once or twice. I find that when this does not suffice, you should hold up your hand in front of the child, much as a traffic cop would do, and face away. Immediately say, "Stop. We do not argue here. The rule is . . . ." If the young person continues to argue, repeat the maneuver with a stated consequence.

If that still does not resolve the situation, walk away. It takes two people to argue, and a child cannot have a one-way argument with himself. Forget trying to get in the last word. I find that when a parent tries to get the last word, it continues the argumentative interaction and accomplishes little or nothing. Remember, when all those about you are losing their heads, keep cool and pretend you are on Mars or in Hawaii. Ignore, ignore, ignore. Just walk away and enforce your rule. If a child follows you and continues to argue, find a safe escape zone such as a restroom in the house or a noisy task such as vacuuming that overrides the clamor.

Establishing consistent rules and making sure there are both positive and negative consequences are important techniques. Several of my young adult patients with ADHD and severe behavioral problems are excessively argumentative. Yet even in the worst-case scenarios, this method works extremely well.

Another frequent concern among parents and teachers is the wiggly child. Many children with Attention Deficit Hyperactivity Disorder use the wiggling mechanism to stay awake and attentive. The behavior is harmless and only an annoyance to people who are intolerant. Parents and teachers need to build tolerance for such behavior and learn to tune it out.

SPECIAL PROBLEMS WITH TEENAGERS

Austin White's mother looked at him on my examining table and shook her head. "I just don't understand him. He had such good control on his medication. Now he won't do what I tell him unless I repeat it several times, just doesn't pay attention. He's moody, wears these weird shirts, and streaks his hair blond. He really has an attitude."

I looked down at the reports from his teachers on my desk. They contained rather good ratings when compared to other children of the same age. One teacher had written clearly in the margin, "Austin is a nice, typical teenage boy."

I smiled and nodded at his mother and said, "He has ETC."

"What?" she asked.

"Early Teenage Crud," I replied.

From roughly age eleven through twenty-one, people go from childhood to being kid-dults, and eventually evolve into adults. A few remain kid-dults for a good part of their lives. At the beginning of this stage children begin to have hormonal changes, so that their bodies grow in length and bulk. Periods in girls and the growth of facial and pubic hair and gradual enlargement of genitals in boys mark kid-dulthood biologically. Along with the physical changes are mood swings, decreased attention span, rebellion, opposition, poor sleep habits, self-centered behavior, and increased risk taking. Kid-dulthood is when young adults test their wings and attempt to declare their independence.

Ah, what is a kid-dult? A kid-dult is a young adult who has many of the physical features of an adult, but maintains the judgment capabilities of a child. Oddly, many children with Attention Deficit Hyperactivity Disorder pass through this phase of development and become less impulsive and hyperactive.

The phase involves many possible experiences that necessitate the use of appropriate judgment and the development of increased responsibility. Among them are driving, dating and sexual interaction, drug and alcohol use, peer influence, and smoking. Rarely is there a totally safe teenager. Peer groups, for better or worse, can and do supersede parental influence. We can only hope that we have given our children enough of a foundation that they can make appropriate choices even when confronted with inappropriate situations.

In many parts of America driving is a rite of passage for most children in middle adolescence. Many schools offer driver's education starting at age fifteen. Most kid-dults have their first obligatory accident within the next two years. A researcher in the Northeast concluded that young adults with ADHD have a much greater risk of automobile accidents. However, his findings were based on a sample of only thirty-five individuals. Furthermore, more than two-thirds of them had been diagnosed as having an oppositional, defiant personality or a conduct disorder, resulting in rebelliousness and a lack of respect for rules and laws. In the years that I practiced general pediatrics with mixed populations, I saw little or no difference in the incidence of car accidents between children without ADHD and those afflicted by the disorder. According to a representative of United States Automobile Association, a major insurance liability company, teenagers in general are a high-risk group. Young adults with Attention Deficit Hyperactivity Disorder are the same as others in this group and don't differ sufficiently to warrant increased insurance rates for their families.

Some simple and important rules to follow regarding driving: Don't sell the family farm and buy a new car. Dents and bruises look a whole lot better on an old clunker of adequate size and without a huge engine. No SUVs. When inexperienced drivers make mistakes and overcorrect, an SUV can roll over easily and become a suicide utility vehicle. A sixteen-year-old cousin of one of my daughters-in-law was recently killed in such an accident. She was an honors student and did not have Attention Deficit Hyperactivity Disorder.

Children under sixteen should not drive alone. Many parents, for their own convenience, will fill out a false affidavit declaring a family emergency so that a fifteen-year-old can get a license and drive independently. One such parent was the wife of a governor of a state that recently legislated a stepwise approach to teen driving. This is a no-no, and frequently portends disaster. Adolescents should drive solo only after their sixteenth birthday, when they have been driving with a reliable adult as a copilot for six months to a year.

In younger adolescents, driving should only be to and from school, religious activities, or work. All teens should contribute something, however small, to the purchase of their car. Direct contribution theoretically makes one a bit more cautious. Young adult drivers should pay for at least part of their insurance and all of their own gasoline. Parents must establish rules of the road in advance and strictly enforce them. If a young adult is at fault in an accident, he should not be permitted to drive by himself for six months. Traffic tickets should be followed by a two-week suspension of driving privileges. If these recur, the penalty should be increased to as much as six months. Mandatory use of seat belts is important. Teens think they are indestructible and many have died needlessly because they did not use seat belts. Failure to use seat belts should result in a suspension of driving privileges for three weeks. Driving under the influence of alcohol or drugs should entail an automatic suspension of the right to drive for at least one year. If there is a repeat offense, complete suspension together with a suitable recovery program is necessary.

In attempts to limit injury and the loss of life caused by teenage driving, the National Transportation Safety Board recommended placing limits on the number of kid-dults below the age of twenty-one who are allowed to be in a car at the same time. Several states have adopted various versions of these guidelines. Distractibility and inattentiveness when more than one teen is in a car increases the chance of a significant accident.

Peer pressure is terrible and frequently overrides many values instilled in kid-dults by their parents. The wish to be part of the "in crowd" can lead to drinking, sex, and violence.

Anna Marie Garcia's mother knew her daughter was going to a teenage party with two friends. It was the first time another teen was driving her to a social event.

"Anna, sometimes things can get out of hand at a party and sometimes the person you are driving with may even take a couple of drinks. When I was a girl I used to keep some 'mad money' in the bottom of my shoe. If these things happen at your party, I want you to call me and I'll come pick you up. If you feel too embarrassed to phone me, use the mad money and take a cab home." She gave the young adult ten dollars to put in the bottom of her shoe.

When Anna Marie saw that two groups of competing adolescents were very upset with each other, she called a cab and came home early. The next morning's newspaper carried a story about a shooting at the same party.

The teen years are the era of raging hormones, which drive the kid-dult to self-stimulation and to want sexual interaction with others. Parents usually frown on teenage sexual interaction. On the other hand, teens in the United States are raised in a culture in which peers, advertisements, TV, music, and magazines transmit messages that unmarried sexual relationships in young adults are common, expected, and often acceptable behaviors. For example, the hit sitcom *Friends* began the 2002 season with an unwed adult's apparent uncertainty as to who fathered her child. For better or worse, emotional maturity in teenagers appears to trail physical maturity by five years, thus setting up kid-dult behavior that often leads to pregnancy and sexually transmitted diseases.

Various surveys report that 20 percent of girls and 30 percent of boys have sexual relationships before age fifteen. By age twenty, 75 percent of American females and 86 percent of American males are sexually active.

According to the United States Centers for Disease Control, the teenage birthrate has declined for the past ten years. However, the rate of unmarried teens having babies and acquiring sexually transmitted diseases in the United States is still much higher than in any other Western industrialized country. There is little difference in the sexual activity in kid-dults in this country and others. Some risk factors for teenage pregnancy are "early dating, drug or alcohol abuse, dropping out of school, lack of a support group or few friends, lack of involvement in school, family, or community activities." Furthermore, perceiving few or no opportunities for success can be devastating.

Young adults with Attention Deficit Hyperactivity Disorder can easily feel isolation both academically and socially. It would be easy for them to slide into a cycle of sex for acceptance, as a means to feel better about themselves. Therefore, it is incumbent upon their families to provide a firm, loving, supportive environment where a teen's strengths are sought out and where effort and trying is rewarded. Parents should stress family and community activities. Parents should seek out youth ministers, rabbis, teachers, and other leaders of young people in the community and work with them to keep the ADHD child attached and included. Keeping children in school and employing appropriate counseling and academic remediation are essential.

Prevention is a key issue. Parents must keep an open line of communication with their teen regarding sex. This is often a difficult and embarrassing task for some parents, but it is essential.

Thirteen-year-old Madison Loeb's mother sat down with her to discuss sex. To her shock, Madison replied, "What do you want to know, Mom?"

Mrs. Loeb raised her eyebrows. "Okay, Madison. Tell me what you understand about sex."

What followed was a stream of misinformation and inaccuracies that had filtered to the thirteen-year-old from other kiddults, television, and other media sources. Mrs. Loeb told her daughter that she was able to get pregnant even at her young age and there was no surefire way to prevent it other than to abstain from intercourse. Although Mrs. Loeb discouraged sexual encounters she discussed and left the door open to talk about contraception at some time in the future, when other needs might arise. She also pointed out that two heterosexual family friends in their mid-twenties had died of AIDS, a viral disease they contracted from sexual encounters in their teens. The Loebs also discussed other sexually transmitted diseases, such as syphilis and gonorrhea, which produces grave illness and may prevent pregnancy later in life. The two of them agreed that there would be no dating other than in chaperoned groups until Madison turned sixteen. No boys were to be in the house without a parent present.

When Madison was a little older, a school-based peer program involving older, popular, and respected teens helped facilitate discussions about feelings and attitudes concerning the appropriate management of physical urges. The group also worked on honing skills through role-playing about how to confront the pressure to become sexually involved.

It is important for male kid-dults to also wait for a time when they are socially mature enough to interact sexually with girls. They too must be responsible for their actions, the results of which unfortunately impact female teenagers more than their male counterparts. Unprotected sex without the use of condoms should be totally prohibited. The same rules that applied to Madison should apply no less to male teens.

It is important for parents to be aware, as far as possible, of where their young adult is, whom they are hanging out with, and what is going on in their house. Parents should set curfews for time spent away from home—nine-thirty to ten on school nights and eleven on weekends, for example, although this may be extended by about an hour in the later teen years.

While privacy issues occur and are important in the teen years, it is equally important to inspect the areas the teen inhabits and works in within the household. In short, know what your kid is doing as much as humanly possible. Such a simple, common practice could have prevented some of the teen shooting rampages that have taken place over the past ten years.

If a kid-dult is running with bad company or engaging in gang activity, don't be afraid to intercede and break it up.

After all is said and done, teenagers with ADHD are not that much different from other young adults. In some ways, other teens have become more like them. Nothing substitutes for family love, support, appropriate guidance, and consistency.

Adults must be role models. If a parent curses all the time, it is likely his or her young adult will use questionable language. Teenagers say curse words for three major reasons: to sound cool and "grown-up," as an expression of anger, and to defy authority. If a parent overreacts, it signals the kid-dult that saying a curse word is a button pusher that can result in parental discomfort and explosiveness. Remember, words are just words. One man's poor choice of language is another man's profession, dialogue, or thing of beauty. "Ass" is a curse word to a teen, but a thing of beauty to a proctologist, a friend to Shreck, or a gold miner. "Hell" may sound bad, but is part of a dialogue and sermon for many pastors, and "damn" is awful sounding from a teen mouthing off, but a colossal work for an engineer. I by no means condone foul language. However, overreacting puts a parent at a disadvantage. As a parent, state clearly that this is unacceptable language, then ignore it, walk away, and go about your business.

An excellent TV spot features a father who finds a kid-dult with marijuana, a few bottles of alcohol, and drug paraphernalia in his room, and asks, "Where did you learn to do this?"

The child soulfully looks at his father and responds, "I learned it from you, Pops, I learned it from you."

Studies have shown that the incidence of drug use in teenagers properly treated for Attention Deficit Hyperactivity Disorder is no greater than in the teenage population at large.

Finally, remember there is also a lot of good in young adults. The transition from child to kid-dult to adult is never easy. Most kids succeed and become fine adults. And believe it or not, most parents survive the transition intact.

TWO

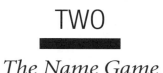

The Name Game

Many parents ask me, "Is ADHD a new disorder?" and "Which does my child have, ADD or ADHD?" Actually, ADHD has been described for more than fifty years, although it has been called by many different names, including ADD.

Heinz Werner and Alfred Strauss worked as clinicians at an institution treating children with severe disabilities in the 1940s. In the course of their work, they also observed a second population, distinct from their more severely affected peers. The children in this second group had trouble learning in some specific areas but were not mentally retarded. Many of these youngsters were also clumsy. They had problems using their large muscles when attempting gross motor activities as well as problems with fine motor coordination, affecting tasks such as cutting, writing, and drawing. However, their disability was not severe enough to be classified as cerebral palsy. In addition, the children had problems with decreased attention span, increased activity levels, and impulsivity.

Werner and Strauss grouped these children into one diagnostic category, using the term Minimal Brain Injury (MBI). They reasoned that, like their more severely affected counterparts, this second cluster of children had an insult to their central nervous system, but one so subtle as to cause less significant manifestations than those seen in the other group.

Werner and Strauss's term was accepted by the medical and education communities to the extent that some clinicians and teachers became "MBI specialists." This terminology prevailed for more than twenty years, until just past the middle of the twentieth century. In an attempt to tone down the idea of actual brain damage implied by the Werner and Strauss nomenclature, an international group of professionals met in Oxford, England. They coined the term Minimal Cerebral Dysfunction (MCD), which, along with Minimal Brain Dysfunction (MBD), became the prevalent designation of the disorder. Under this umbrella the specialists in the field attempted to explain the overlapping and intertwined cognitive (learning), behavioral, and neurological problems displayed by these children. In the United States, a steering committee sponsored by the National Society of Crippled Children and Adults, in association with a division of the Public Health Service, convened a meeting to discuss issues related to children with Minimal Cerebral Dysfunction.

This definition lasted until the great turf wars of the late 1960s and 1970s. During this era, various groups of professionals began the process of dissecting the child into various component parts, rather than taking a holistic, full-child approach. Children were divided into educational, neuromedical, and behavioral rubrics.

In 1972, at the Advanced Study Institute, a conference of education experts held at Northwestern University, fifteen special educators constructed an educational definition of learning disabilities. In essence, they teased out a cognitive child from the existing multidisciplinary definitions such as Minimal Cerebral Dysfunction.

In an earlier paper, Corrine Kass and Helmer Myklebust, prominent professionals in the field of special education, urged the teaching community to focus on the scholastic and cognitive portions of Minimal Cerebral Dysfunction. They proposed that a group of children existed who were of normal, near normal, or above normal intelligence, but had significantly discrepant learning in areas such as reading, math, spelling, written language, and auditory comprehension. When Dr. Samuel Kirk, a pioneer in the field of learning disabilities, addressed a meeting of parents of children with these differences and said the children acted as though they were "learning disabled," a new term arose.

Many professionals in this era believed it was of little importance to know the cause of the child's problems or if learning and social interactions also were affected. Most efforts were focused on getting an educational diagnosis and constructing an educational plan of remediation aimed at specific problems.

In the late 1960s and early 1970s, the individual states determined what constituted a severe discrepancy for purposes of special education. Thus, children in Texas could get services in school if their standard scores (I.Q. equivalency) on achievement tests in areas such as reading, math, and writing were sixteen points below the intelligence quotient, whereas children in New York could not get services until the differential between achievement and intellect reached thirty-two points.

Many medical and other professionals denied that these children had a disability or problem of any kind. They reasoned that even though the children were less capable of learning under the usual classroom circumstances, there was no real problem, only differences of learning and behavioral styles.

About the same time, developmental pediatricians focused on the medical-neurological aspects of these children. These professionals used the term Hyperkinetic Syndrome.

Members of the psychiatric community initially became involved in this dilemma in the 1970s as well. They constructed a manual to codify various mental illnesses. This initial effort, published by the American Psychiatric Association (APA), was called the *Diagnostic and Statistical Manual of Mental Disorders*, second edition (*DSM*-II). Several years later, in the third edition (*DSM*-III), they created elaborate definitions of all kinds of mental illness.

In essence, *DSM*-III became the accepted, authorized text for connecting groups of behavioral symptoms into various psychiatric disorders. Within the group Disruptive Disorders of Childhood, a committee of psychiatrists, psychologists, and other professionals included a new diagnostic category called Attention Deficit Disorder (ADD), claiming that the most prominent symptom these children displayed was the inability to pay attention. Four types of the disorder were described: Attention Deficit Disorder with Hyperactivity (ADD-H); Attention Deficit Disorder without Hyperactivity (ADD–no H); Attention Deficit Disorder, Combined, for children with a combination of attentional problems, hyperactivity, and impulsivity (ADD-C); and Attention Deficit Disorder, Residual (ADD-R), which was used to describe young adults who had hyperactivity as children, but in whom that aspect of their problem disappeared in the teen years. The symptoms had to be present before the age of seven and for at least six months.

Little mention was made of learning problems, executive function (self-monitoring, organizational, and sequencing skills), or social interaction. However, the concept of Attention Deficit Disorder certainly had some merit, and it rapidly caught on with the public and commercial drug companies.

In 1987 the APA published the *Diagnostic and Statistical Manual*, third edition–revised (*DSM*-III-R). The entire formulation of Attention Deficit Disorder was turned upside down. No longer were there separate categories for children with inattention only. Individual hyperactive and residual types were completely deleted. Rather, all children were lumped under one categorical diagnosis called Attention Deficit Hyperactivity Disorder. Sixteen diagnostic criteria were listed. If a child had eight of the disordered behaviors to a greater extent than his peers, he qualified as having a problem. Some signs had to be present for more than six months and before the age of seven.

This idea was terribly flawed. For one thing, many children had trouble with inattention only, yet were stigmatized by this diagnosis as being hyperactive and impulsive. Another problem was that a child could be significantly disordered in six areas, sufficient to interfere with scholastic or social performance, yet not meet the diagnostic criteria. Once again, executive function, cognitive processing, and social interaction were mentioned only in passing.

In 1988 and 1989, during the amendment process for Public Law 94-142 (Education for All Handicapped Children Act), the U.S. House of Representatives passed legislation that made Attention Deficit Disorder a separate and distinct handicapping category. Much of the impetus for this issue came from the parents group CHADD (Children and Adults with Attention Deficit Disorder).

ADHD: The Great Misdiagnosis

Fearing that the professional community interpreted this diagnosis so loosely that it would saturate the public school special education system, the Senate Committee on Education did not endorse a separate category. Instead, it held meetings that explored the subject with prominent professionals, advocacy groups, and parents of children with ADHD.

What lawmakers found was a mix of often conflicting and divergent viewpoints as to what Attention Deficit Hyperactivity Disorder was, as well as a hesitation by many educational professionals to include the disorder as a separate handicap category under the law. The government queried several national organizations and individuals on the nature of ADHD and whether it should be considered a separate legal category. The AAP deemed that Attention Deficit Hyperactivity Disorder was a group of disorders that caused persistent dysfunction in the central nervous system in the areas of attending (alertness), activity (motion), cognitive processing (learning), executive function (sequencing, organizational skills, self-monitoring), and social interaction (see Appendix 2 for full text). It listed parameters of these and associated problems. Furthermore, it stated that behaviors occurred along a continuum from normal variance, to a problem in a single environment, to a full-blown disorder that involved most areas of a child's life, such as school, home, day care, and play (however, since young adults are seldom involved in day care, the workplace environment should be substituted when applicable). In addition, it pointed out that problems in learning and other areas, including medical problems, could frequently simulate ADHD symptoms and yet be something completely different.

In 1996, when the *Diagnostic and Statistical Manual*, fourth edition (*DSM*-IV), appeared, the diagnostic criteria changed once again. Although the term Attention Deficit Hyperactivity Disorder was retained, three distinct categories were listed: ADHD, Predominantly Inattentive Type; ADHD, Predominantly Hyperactive-Impulsive Type; and, if symptoms were present across all categories, ADHD, Combined Type. Confronted with all these new categories, many professionals wondered why the APA couldn't admit it made a nomenclature mistake in *DSM*-III-R and revert to its first and more functional definition. The term ADHD, Predominantly Inattentive, has to be one of the greatest oxymorons of all time. These children are neither disruptive, hyperactive, nor impulsive.

DSM-IV listed several behavioral traits in each of the three ADHD categories (see Appendices 1 and 2 for the entire list). A person had to display six of the traits to a significant degree in order to be classified within the Inattentive or the Hyperactive-Impulsive category, or six from each of the two main groupings (for a total of twelve) to be considered as having the combined disorder. To their credit, the APA writers made some very important progress in a series of disclaimers. One key change emphasized the need for clinical significance before a person could be considered disordered. For example, if a child had a cluster of these symptoms but maintained school performance expected for his intelligence, had friends, and functioned adequately at play or work and in the home environment, he could not be considered as having a disorder.

A few years ago, I was consulted about Michael Cox, age nine. He had an above average intellect, did well in his scout troop, made the honor roll in a high-performance private school, and had many friends. At home his behavior and interaction with his parents and siblings were normal for his age.

Michael's teacher told his parents, however, that Michael had many of the symptoms of ADHD and that he could perform better if he took medication. Mr. and Mrs. Cox took the boy to a physician who saw him for less than ten minutes and prescribed Ritalin. Then they brought Michael to me for a second opinion. Inasmuch as he clearly performed above expected levels in all of his environments and was not disordered, I recommended he not start any medication. The last time I spoke to the Coxes, Michael was eleven years old and was continuing to perform well in school and outside activities.

The APA made another significant advance over its prior proposals. ADHD could not occur in isolated settings. They stipulated that the symptoms needed to be present in two or more environments of function, including play, school, day care, and home for younger children, or school, socialization, work, and home for young adults and adults.

In the earlier *Diagnostic and Statistical Manuals*, ADHD could coexist with any number of mental illness disorders. In *DSM*-IV, the APA acknowledged that symptoms associated with ADHD could also be found with various other neurobehavioral and developmental disorders such as autism, as well as with schizophrenia and other psychoses (mental illness marked by hallucinations, delusions, and flights of thought). Furthermore, *DSM*-IV declared that the symptom complex of increased activity, inattention, and impulsivity could be called ADHD only when not better explained by other problems, such as mood disorders (depression and sadness disorders), anxiety (worrying about everything in an abnormal way), personality disorders such as oppositional defiant disorders (purposefully being rebellious and refusing to do what is reasonably requested), and dissociative personality disorders (e.g., multiple personalities). However, it did not go far enough. *DSM-IV* failed to state that the symptoms at times might also be better explained by various disorders of the special senses (eyesight and hearing), some medical problems, psychosocial problems (e.g., abuse, neglect, and chaotic family relationships between parents), and various learning disorders.

In 1997, the year following the publication of *DSM*-IV, the AAP published basically the same codifications, aimed at primary care doctors. The definition of Attention Deficit Hyperactivity Disorder in this document included most but not all the features of the 1991 definition that was written by the AAP Committee on Children with Disabilities and presented before the working group of the U.S. Senate (see Appendix 2 for the definition).

In the last several years, various developmentalists have challenged the idea that attention is the dominating problem in these children. Dr. Paul Dworkin, a developmental pediatrician and professor of pediatrics at the University of Connecticut in Hartford, recently expressed concerns that the present concept of ADHD as primarily a deficit of attention is flawed. He pointed out, among other things, that this conception fails to take into account the learning and behavioral problems that these children frequently experience, or their difficulties with self-monitoring.

Many behavioral scientists, neurologists, parents, educators, and pediatricians would like to see a name for the disorder that would better capture all of the varied problems these children have.

Through it all, the children will exhibit the same sorts of symptoms. Only the name for the disorder will change.

THREE

The Real Thing

If so many conditions display the same symptoms, does Attention Deficit Hyperactivity Disorder really exist as a significant separate entity?

When a child exhibits inattention, increased activity, or impulsivity, or any combination thereof, a clinician must consider these behaviors as symptoms of any number of disorders. In short, these symptoms are to neurobehavioral disorders as fever is to other illnesses. A person does not have a fever disorder. Rather, the fever signifies that something is askew, and the clinician must determine the cause of the fever.

The symptoms of ADHD may be present in more than thirty other disorders, ranging from problems with the sensory systems, to mental illness, to scholastic, psychosocial, and medical problems. It is very important to know the exact cause of the symptoms, since many of these disorders require different forms of medication and remediation (the process of curing, helping, correcting, or overcoming disabilities or problems). Indeed, some of the medications and techniques used to treat one disorder might make a different disorder worse. Therefore, much as one searches for the cause of a fever, the detective work must be aimed at finding an accurate diagnosis for the true problem causing inattention, hyperactivity, and impulsivity in any given individual.

The children who have true neurogenic ADHD—which is rooted in the central nervous system—are the same cluster of children that was previously diagnosed as having Minimal Brain Injury, Minimal Cerebral Dysfunction, Hyperkinetic Syndrome, and ADD. These children fall into two predominant sets of circumstances: one is genetic, and the other is related to damage to the central nervous system and brain. The genetic group probably composes 40 percent of the true ADHD cases. For this group, there is a strong family history of a parent, a grandparent, or primary relatives with the symptoms of ADHD.

One lecturer recently noted that we might have more ADHD cases in the United States than elsewhere because many of our ancestors came to these shores after they left more secure environments. After all, a person had to be a bit impulsive to travel on a small ship thousands of miles across a vast and dangerous ocean to an unknown place. People had to go against the known traditions of the time; they had to want change. Some of our ancestors settled the New World from the jails of England or were outcasts from other traditional societies. A number of our founding fathers ran rum against the British blockades. And those fellows who threw all that tea into Boston Harbor did not exactly walk between the lines. Many of our predecessors were a restless lot. They were unrealistic dreamers who had a way of getting things done, at times in unconventional ways. Crossing the prairies, mountains, and wilderness in small horse-driven wagons to settle the land from ocean to ocean required some risk taking and kinetic drive. More recently, the Mariel boat people arrived in south Florida from the jails and asylums of Cuba.

The Real Thing

Children with a genetic basis for ADHD have incorrect wiring or poor connections between the nerve cells that make up the brain. This deficit is much like a slightly flawed telephone switching station. Most of the messages get through to the correct place. However, a few calls get routed to places they were never meant to go. These misconnections cause problems in how the brain carries messages and interprets information, particularly in the areas of paying attention, modulating activity, being organized, doing things in sequence, linking one piece of information to another, connecting facts to make meaning, interpreting social signals in all environments, and responding to the feelings of others.

First-degree relatives (mothers, fathers, brothers, or sisters) of these children appear to have a 25 percent risk of a similar problem. Nearly two thousand pairs of twins were studied in Australia. The incidence of ADHD among the twins was between 11 and 12 percent, and was only 8 percent in other siblings. Interestingly enough, 83 percent of the identical twins (from the same egg) had exactly the same subtype of ADHD (either Predominantly Inattentive, Predominantly Hyperactive-Impulsive, or Combined).

Very recently the national genome project discovered that some people with ADHD have an increased amount of material on a gene on the eleventh human chromosome. This important discovery may lead not only to a better understanding of ADHD, but also to a test to identify the type of ADHD transmitted genetically from parents to their children.

Recently I saw a child in our clinic with symptoms of ADHD, mostly in the inattentive quadrant. Her dad accompanied her to the office and gave us her family's history.

"I don't know why Sara's teachers and mother are so worried," he said. "I was exactly the same way in school myself. Damn nearly failed. Now I'm the CEO of a major corporation listed on the New York Stock Exchange. My high energy actually helped me in business more than it hurt me." Further history revealed that Sara's grandfather had four brothers, only one of whom finished high school in the 1920s. They were all extremely spirited and energetic people. Three of the five became very successful businessmen.

This is not an isolated story. Many parents and grandparents tell me they have the same kinds of problems with attention and activity that their children and grandchildren do. Unfortunately, many of them struggled in school academically and with interpersonal relationships. Not all of them had the good outcome related to me by Sara's father.

Different from this first group of children, who have a genetic basis for their ADHD, is a second group of children who received subtle damage to the central nervous system and brain. Although Werner and Strauss of the Minimal Brain Injury theory were scoffed at for more than twenty years as being too harsh in their definition, this cluster of children persists. In fact, their numbers are increasing.

About the time I first entered pediatrics in the early 1960s, the wife of President John F. Kennedy gave birth to a premature baby who was rather large by today's standards. The infant developed trouble breathing because its lungs were immature. There was little that could be done in that era to help the infant survive, and Patrick died several days after his birth. Because of advances in medicine and technology, babies born today at three pounds eight ounces and below are surviving with regularity. Mothers who carry only to the twenty-sixth week are having babies who frequently live, because of modern technology and the skills of neonatologists. Just this month I saw a fourteen-ounce survivor who at age six had severe learning disabilities and significant problems with attention span, hyperactivity, and impulse control.

Many of these babies have hemorrhages of varying sizes in the brain. Others have difficulty with how the blood vessels form in part of the eye (the retina), developing a condition known as retinopathy of prematurity. Most have problems with immature lungs and must be supported with ventilator machines for prolonged periods of time. If sufficiently severe, these breathing difficulties can deprive their brains of oxygen for varying periods of time. Sometimes their blood must receive oxygen from sources outside their own bodies. More than half of brain growth occurs from the twenty-fifth week of gestation on—particularly growth in that part of the brain involved with areas of higher learning, such as reading and the interpretation of sounds.

None of this goes on inside the mother's uterus, but must occur through artificial means in sort of a supplemental, technological placenta. Various breathing machines give extra oxygen, medicines control blood pressure, and intravenous solutions sustain at least part of nutrition.

Premature babies with very low birth weight may stop breathing for brief periods of time (apnea) and their heart rates may become precariously slow. They may develop transient hypothyroidism. Furthermore, their livers may act immaturely, failing to dissolve a substance called bilirubin; this can stain the skin with a yellow pigment and, if severe enough, can poison the brain. In addition, these babies are forced to survive in a stressful environment that includes unpleasant and sometimes painful treatments from their caretakers in order to save their lives. They suffer decreased interrelationships with their mothers, constant noise, and bright lighting.

ADHD: The Great Misdiagnosis

It was feared for a long time that most of these babies would be severely damaged, resulting in cerebral palsy or mental retardation. In reality only relatively few become this handicapped. However, many of them eventually have more subtle problems with learning, such as expressive and receptive language problems, learning disabilities, and symptoms of decreased attention span, impulsivity, and increased activity levels. Low birth weight is an independent risk factor for ADHD. A recent article estimated that as many as 50 percent of low-birth-weight children have trouble learning or have ADHD. In addition, 25 to 30 percent are affected by psychiatric disorders at adolescence.

Dr. Adan Bhutta and his associates from the University of Arkansas at Little Rock analyzed data from fifteen different studies that compared three thousand premature and term babies at five years of age. His group concluded that premature infants are at a higher risk of developing ADHD in childhood than those born at term.

Luis and Nancy Gomez expected their first child on July 3. Instead, at one o'clock in the morning on April 1, Nancy went into hard labor and Luis immediately drove her to the hospital. Nancy's obstetrician attempted to use drugs to prevent her from delivering so early. However, the procedure did not work, and on April 2 she delivered a two-pound, two-ounce baby boy whom the family named José.

José's skin was blue when he was born, and almost immediately he showed signs of difficulty breathing. Doctors put a tube that was attached to a respirator machine down his trachea. A catheter placed in an artery in José's belly button supplied him with medicine and fluids. All sorts of wires connected him to an array of monitors that measured his pulse, respiratory rate, blood pressure, oxygen, and carbon dioxide. He inhaled a chemical called surfactant that lubricated his tiny lung sacs to help him breathe better. He remained on the respirator for twelve days. When José was discharged several weeks later at four pounds four ounces, a neurologist examined him and declared that he was normal.

José's language development and motor skills (sitting, walking, etc.) lagged behind those of his peers by a couple of months. However, Mr. and Mrs. Gomez were reassured by their pediatrician that this was normal in small premature babies. In time, José did catch up with the other kids in his neighborhood, except that he was a bit difficult to understand at times.

A few weeks after José entered kindergarten, his teacher had a conference with the Gomezes and informed them that their son had a poor attention span and problems with writing and handling numbers. He still had difficulty pronouncing words, and the school recommended speech therapy. When José reached the middle of first grade, an educational diagnostician tested him and found normal intelligence, but learning difficulties in math, reading, and writing.

In 1997, a study at Columbia University in New York looked at low-birth-weight infants at age six. Almost 16 percent of this group had ADHD.

In Canada, children who had weighed two pounds or less at birth were tested at eight and sixteen years of age. They had significant problems in reading, writing, and math, with math performance the worst. Behavior checklists were also used with these children. However, according to Dr. Saroj Saigol, the lead investigator, this data is still being analyzed and the results are still not available.

Similar children in Michigan were studied at eight years of age. Those who did not have diseased lungs that failed to clear adequately, a condition called bronchopulmonary dysplasia (BPD), had average intelligence in the mid-nineties (normal) and learning problems in math. However, children who suffered from BPD had borderline intelligence (I.Q.'s in the eighties) and serious disabilities in reading and especially in math.

Such difficulties are not just limited to surviving small infants. Diseases such as leukemia in childhood, which was virtually a death sentence when I was a resident in the 1960s, are now curable in a great many children. During their treatment, most children receive medicine into their central nervous system and radiation to the head. Increasing subsets of school-age children with learning differences and ADHD are coming from this cluster. Moreover, advances in technology and the improved skills of doctors who specialize in pediatric intensive care have given us survivors not before possible in cases of head injury, near drowning, and meningitis—all of which add to this group.

Lastly, we have an epidemic of drug and alcohol use in the United States that is only superficially revealed. Even young women who are not addicted to drugs and alcohol may be at risk for having a baby with fetal alcohol or drug effects. Many do not realize they are pregnant until they have missed periods for two months or more. By that time two-thirds of the crucial first trimester of fetal development has taken place. In short, women of childbearing age who are trying to have babies or are practicing unprotected sex should never take drugs or drink alcohol.

In addition, many drinking and drug habits are unknown to the mother's physician or the outside world. They remain in the closet with the door tightly closed. A survey taken in one Texas county several years ago revealed that only two mothers of newborn babies admitted to drinking alcohol while they were pregnant. Some mothers state they had an alcohol or drug habit before they knew they were pregnant and stopped cold turkey. It is very unlikely that this can occur quickly without a treatment plan. A few others will reluctantly admit the problem only when a child displays problems in learning or with ADHD symptoms.

Grandparents frequently raise these children because the parents abuse alcohol and illicit substances to excess and desert or neglect the children. Some children of alcohol abusers show signs of full-blown fetal alcohol syndrome, which include a small head, retarded growth, thin lips, small eyes, a flattening of the facial area, a scooped nose with a wide bridge, and low-set ears. However, more usually there are subtle problems with development of the nervous system, and these result in decreased attention span, hyperactivity, impulsive behavior, and learning difficulties.

Signs that a mother abused drugs during pregnancy may not be obvious. However, some newborns show symptoms of withdrawal. Many children who were exposed to drug abuse before birth show rapidly cycling combinations of hyperactivity, impulsivity, and inattention. Frequently, the usual medical regimens are not very effective in treating these children.

Jacob Henderson was born to a mother who intermittently abused cocaine and alcohol during her pregnancy. As an infant he was extremely fussy, cried almost continuously, couldn't be consoled, and had problems with feeding. Other than somewhat thin lips, Jacob had no physical signs of maternal alcohol or drug abuse. Jacob's mother continued her cocaine and alcohol habit and frequently neglected her child. When he was three months old, Child Protective Services removed him from his mother's home and placed him with his maternal grandmother, Mrs. Sterling. His behavior in childhood was very erratic. When school began, Jacob was hyperactive, inattentive, and disorganized, and he had difficulty with all aspects of learning. Testing in a developmental center revealed that Jacob was a slow learner with problems in reading, written language, and math. The center also made a diagnosis of ADHD.

More than 45,000 children a year in the United States are exposed to cocaine during their mother's pregnancy. Tests with animals have revealed a link between such cocaine exposure and problems with selective attention skills. The link may extend to areas such as socialization and learning ability.

FOUR

The Imitators

Many problems, disorders, and illnesses have similar symptoms to ADHD: hearing and vision abnormalities, allergies, neurological problems, mental retardation, problems with learning and school, various medical illnesses, autism disorders, depression, and family alterations or disruptions. This chapter examines some of these ADHD look-alikes.

HEARING AND VISION

Lekisha Wright, a bright-eyed, happy little girl, began first grade with great enthusiasm and childhood joy. Mrs. Jones, her teacher, seated her in the next-to-last row in a classroom of twenty children. After two weeks of school, it became obvious to Mrs. Jones that Lekisha was not paying attention, seemed antsy, and could not follow directions. She asked the little girl's mother to come in for a conference.

Mrs. Jones told Mrs. Wright that Lekisha was very restless, could not follow what was going on in the classroom, was not alert, and just couldn't do what was requested. "I was at a teachers seminar recently," Mrs. Jones said, "and Lekisha sounds like some of the children they described. You really need to take her to your doctor and see if she has ADHD."

Fortunately, the child's physician, a general pediatrician in our clinic, was astute. One of the first things she did was check Lekisha's hearing and vision. Sure enough, the child had moderate hearing loss in both ears. Further testing revealed that the hearing loss was from a mild infection and fluid behind both eardrums. After a course of appropriate treatment, Lekisha's hearing returned to normal, her problem was resolved, and she made splendid progress during the remainder of the first grade.

Any child who has symptoms similar to Lekisha's should be tested for a hearing or vision problem as part of any workup. Such problems are frequently mistaken for ADHD, Predominantly Inattentive. If a child has severe problems with vision or hearing, one would hope that a clinician would find the problem long before the child begins school. However, a mild to moderate visual or hearing impairment can go unnoticed. If a child with a moderate, undiagnosed visual or hearing impairment gets placed in the back or middle of a classroom, she may eventually be accused of not paying attention or following directions.

Many hospitals now check children for hearing loss from the time they are born. The AAP and other national organizations suggest that hearing and vision be formally tested from age three. Informal testing of vision, hearing, and language development should be done with each well baby and child visit. If your physician does not do this testing, you should request that it be done.

PROBLEMS WITH LEARNING AND SCHOOL
Learning Disabilities or Differences

One day I received a phone call from one of my colleagues, Dr. Charles Smith. He related that his daughter, Allison, was having a terrible time in second grade at her private parochial school. In order to properly evaluate the child, my group asked her parents and teachers to fill out very comprehensive history forms. The family was asked questions about Allison's birth, her mother's history during pregnancy, where the family lived, Allison's early development, her other family members and their interactions, her behavioral and academic characteristics, past illnesses or health problems, and her behaviors at home.

A questionnaire sent to the school sought information about her scholastic ability relative to her peers in many areas, including reading, math, spelling, writing, and self-expression. Some questions explored her demeanor and actions in the classroom and her relationships with teachers and peers.

Allison's parental history did not reveal any problems with increased activity, decreased attention span, impulsivity, or other behavioral aberrations at home. Her teachers indicated that she was performing below or markedly below expected levels in several academic areas. They estimated her intelligence at above average and couldn't understand why she did not perform better.

Because Allison's problem occurred in only one environment—the classroom—I asked her parents to request intelligence and achievement testing from her local school system. Allison was a student at a private school, but the law requires local school districts to evaluate private school children when a significant academic problem arises. When she completed the testing, it was obvious that Allison had a severe learning disability in reading, reading comprehension, and written language.

Unfortunately, Allison's school refused to modify her regular assignments or provide tutors or other forms of special help. Allison eventually changed to a school that offered her the special assistance she needed. Combined with some additional tutoring and good parental support, she progressed nicely in her new school.

Allison did not need any form of medication to help her, just appropriate educational placement and adequate services. She is just one of many children whose stories cross my desk every year. These children are handicapped when schools—private or public—fail to provide the support they need.

Usually only 10 to 40 percent of children with learning disabilities or differences have ADHD. Conversely, 40 to 60 percent of children with true neurogenic ADHD have learning disabilities. Therefore, it is not surprising that problems with cognitive processing were included as a part of the AAP's definition of ADHD.

Children with either a learning difficulty or an intelligence quotient between seventy and eighty-five (slow learner) frequently have problems with attention span in the classroom because they simply do not understand the material presented to them. Imagine sitting in a classroom in China without having any knowledge of the language. After a while, you would not pay attention, because you would not understand any of the material. In time, you might even become restless or overactive. If the frustration became overwhelming, you might even strike out in an impulsive, angry way toward others in the classroom.

Some children faced with such frustrations become the class clown, for no one really expects much from a clown. Many fail to turn in assignments. These children are usually told that they don't follow instructions, or that they have a poor attitude. Under the ridicule of their peers, they eventually stop trying to complete work in the classroom altogether. Children don't want to look like a failure in front of their peers. To avoid producing flawed material that might be criticized or laughed at, some children don't produce anything. Even multiple grades of zero wouldn't stop this catch-22 behavior.

These learning difficulties are not ADHD, and medication would offer little help. When medication substitutes for academic help, it is like covering a festering abscess with a tiny bandage. In time, the sore grows larger and creates greater problems in the end. Failure to properly identify learning differences only causes suffering, academic failure, ridicule, and defeat.

Few if any teachers can properly estimate a child's potential or intelligence without the benefit of educational testing. Many parents are informed that their youngsters are very bright when actually they are capable of only average or below-average work. Conversely, teachers may underestimate a young person's true intellectual potential. No child with problems in the academic arena should ever be evaluated for or placed on medication without adequate, comprehensive, and appropriate educational testing to identify a problem such as a learning disability.

In March 1999, the Department of Pediatrics at the University of Connecticut in Hartford reported that, of 245 children referred to their service for ADHD, 91 percent were diagnosed with various learning disorders, but only 38 percent actually had the disorder.

What many parents and various professionals think is ADHD may instead be a problem with learning.

Gifted Children

Lucy Nyguen usually made straight A's, but her report card was filled with "unsatisfactories" and "needs improvement" in conduct and work habits. At a conference with Lucy's teacher, her mother was told that Lucy had a short attention span, got out of her seat frequently, and did drawings instead of her daily lessons. Quite distressed, Mrs. Nyguen took Lucy to a psychologist. He tested the girl and found an I.Q. of 135. Furthermore, on achievement tests Lucy was two to three years ahead of her classmates in nearly all subjects. Lucy already knew all the classroom material and didn't feel she had to pay attention to information that she had already acquired. Like learning-disabled students, gifted children may experience the frustration of an inappropriate classroom placement.

Gifted children in a regular classroom setting are frequently labeled as hyperactive or inattentive. Their learning style tends to be kinetic. Because they already know much of the material being taught in the class, they may pay little attention to the teacher's instructional efforts. Their minds wander to other things.

Behaviorally, gifted children can be a challenge because a simple "No" may not suffice. A gifted student frequently wants to know, "Why not?" Challenging the teacher, or instigating knowledge and intelligence battles with the teacher, can become a daily routine. It takes a teacher with special talent to handle this kind of child and get performance up to intellectual capacity.

Such children do quite well in advanced classes. When these are not accessible, modifying the classroom routine to a higher level of performance for the child is helpful. The teacher might ask the child to do an errand in order to vary the classroom experience. Being firm and not threatened by a mind that constantly questions is paramount.

Parental Expectation Inconsistent with a Child's Abilities

Kelsey Doge was the son of an aeronautical engineer and a mother who had a Ph.D. in psychology. Because of their own intellectual status they expected Kelsey to be able to attend a school that required its students to learn two years above their normal grade placement level. This included a great deal of pressure to perform advanced academics in the classroom, as well as an extensive load of homework every evening.

Kelsey brought home borderline and failing grades. His teachers complained that he did not pay attention during lessons and that his written output was poor. He only passed with extensive tutoring and by going to summer school each year. His parents felt that because they were able to excel at school, Kelsey too should do well, even in a fast-moving academic environment.

The boy was taken to a pediatrician, who made a diagnosis of ADHD based on a Conners form (a questionnaire evaluating ADHD symptoms). She immediately put Kelsey on Ritalin. The child continued to have problems, to the extent that frustration led to emotional outbursts at school and at home. Finally, the physician referred the child to a psychologist. He administered a group of educational tests, and concluded that Kelsey had a normal intelligence quotient of 100. In short, he could progress in a regular school without frustration, but had difficulty when placed in a classroom with children with I.Q.'s above 120 who worked two years above his level.

Unfortunately, the Doges were convinced that their son was brighter than the psychologist suggested, had ADHD, and with different or increasing doses of medication could do better at the private school. Because of their own egos, they preferred that their child be on medication, struggling in an advanced private school, rather than succeed in a normally structured classroom, without the need for medical intervention.

I am also sometimes confronted by parents whose child has an average I.Q. and who is not making A's in most academic subjects. They suggest that their child is not performing up to their expectations because of ADHD. Such parents do not accept the fact that the intellectual potential of their child is in the B and C range. Frequently, such parents put tremendous pressure on clinicians to start their child on a stimulant medication.

It is unethical for parents to demand or for physicians to prescribe Ritalin and related medications for enhancement of academic performance under these circumstances. These demands are in the same category as prescribing steroids to bulk up athletes in competitive sports.

Dysgraphia

One of my patients, Dakota Cohen, did extremely well in kindergarten and in the first and second grades. When he reached the third and fourth grades, however, his parents began to receive complaints from his teachers that he did not finish his work or complete tests. Homework became an arduous chore, taking two to three hours as Dakota tried to complete unfinished class work as well as his usual homework load. A battle of wills ensued between Dakota and his parents, with a great deal of shouting, punishment, cajoling, and manipulation.

Fearing he had a problem with attention span and could not complete his work because of decreased alertness and a wandering mind, Mr. and Mrs. Cohen took their son to a Dallas developmental clinic for a complete evaluation. Testing revealed that his intelligence was slightly greater than average, and his capacity for reading and math coincided with his overall abilities. However, on the Children's Handwriting Evaluation Scale (CHES), a standardized test for writing ability, Dakota performed at less than the eighth percentile for motor speed (ability to write material neatly in a timely manner). He also had trouble with motor memory, which was demonstrated by many substitutions of letters and words. In other words, when required to give a written response to a reading assignment, what might take the average student five minutes to complete would take Dakota fifteen or twenty minutes.

The CHES revealed that Dakota had dysgraphia—difficulties with writing. Children with dysgraphia cannot write neatly without really thinking which way their fingers need to position themselves. This becomes an exhausting task, involving continuous conscious thought and mechanical concentration.

Imagine driving a car along one of the routes you regularly travel. You know the route so well that your driving is automatic. You can pay attention to what your children in the backseat are saying because you don't have to concentrate on the details of steering. Now imagine that a storm suddenly arises, creating darkness, thunder, and lightning. You can hardly see in the downpour. You have to concentrate. You tell the children to be quiet. Your thinking has changed from automatic to cognitive. You need to carefully process each little move you make. This is far more tiring and tedious than automatic thinking. You emerge from the storm tired and perhaps irritable.

Children with dysgraphia encounter this on a daily basis. For them writing becomes an arduous chore. When a child writes or talks, there is a steady, even flow, with little expenditure of energy. Boys and girls with dysgraphia have to really think and work hard to get print or cursive writing on paper, and this constant thought tasking becomes exhausting. When they copy material from the blackboard or overheads, the results are often incomplete. Being unable to take complete notes during a classroom lecture leads to inadequate information and obvious gaps in learning.

Several components go into the ability to write, including being able to form letters in their proper perspective, not upside down or backwards. Other factors are competent eye–hand coordination, the ability of the brain to send signals to the fingers to tell them exactly how to move in an automatic fashion to form letters and numbers, appropriate slant, proper spacing, and sufficient fine motor coordination. Children with dysgraphia frequently have problems with one or more of these components.

One neurological sign of dysgraphia is finger agnosia, or the inability to identify where fingers are in space. Other signs are unusual holding of a pencil—for example, using four instead of three fingers—poor duplication of finger placements, and poor copying. Treatment for dysgraphia frequently involves bypass strategies. Learning how to use word processing, for example, appreciably helps the problem. After all, the letter B always looks the same on a computer and is located in the same position, the printer always turns out neat copy, and the spelling function helps get words in shape. However, some children with dysgraphia have difficulty knowing where their fingers are in space, so they may have to alternate looking at the monitor and then the keyboard. Another helpful strategy that teachers use is giving extra time on written tests and assignments. If necessary, a child with dysgraphia should be tested orally.

When a child has to copy from overheads or a chalk- or marker board, a printed handout is helpful. In these situations, as well as when notes from lectures become important, another student can act as a peer note taker to assist the child with dysgraphia. Tape recorders may also be used when appropriate. Large blocks of written material should be broken down into smaller subsets. For example, when a dysgraphic child is presented with fifty problems on a page he may become overwhelmed and not complete any of the material. On the other hand, presenting five to ten problems at a time and then going on to the next group may lead to success. Teachers should also decrease written homework load for these students.

Mental Retardation

Several other problems can appear to be ADHD but are actually from other causes. One of these is mental retardation (MR). Children with mental retardation, defined as an intellect below seventy on standardized intelligence tests, should be readily identified, especially when a child has moderate to severe MR. Although some of their behaviors may seem similar to ADHD, they are really from other sources. In children with an I.Q. below fifty-five, many of the medications that work for children with true neurogenic ADHD are not beneficial. As with other children who experience problems in the regular classroom setting, children with mental retardation need the appropriate educational placement.

However, detection of children with mild mental retardation, in the sixty to sixty-nine range, is more difficult. Martin Engle was held back in kindergarten because his teacher said his pre-reading and writing skills lagged behind. In the second grade his teacher said he was very smart, but not trying. He was referred to a counselor who did a short test for ADHD. Based on this instrument his parents were told to take him to a doctor in order to begin medication, as he clearly had ADHD.

However, his mother sensed that there was something terribly wrong with the way Martin learned at school. Therefore, she sought help at a center that specialized in neurodevelopmental and behavioral disorders. Testing revealed that the boy was mildly mentally retarded, with an I.Q. of sixty-five. He is currently getting special education services and is making progress.

Personality Conflicts

Conflicts within a classroom can raise havoc with how a student functions. Children will at times have disputes with other children; some will goad or bully others. Some young people are susceptible to overstimulation. If two of these children sit next to one another, disruptions may result. When such children are seated at a distance from each other, the entire problem may dissipate. Severe friction between children within a classroom can lead to behaviors that can be interpreted as impulsivity or inattention.

Every now and then a personality conflict will evolve between a teacher and a particular student. If only one teacher among several considers a child disruptive, inattentive, impulsive, or socially maladaptive, then the possibility of a teacher–student conflict should be explored.

One of the worst cases of classroom friction that I encountered in my clinical practice occurred with a boy named Robbie Snead, whose mother was teaching at the same school he attended. The year before Mrs. Snead had a bitter dispute with her colleague, Ms. Medders, over curriculum and overall philosophy. In the new school year, Robbie Snead became a student in Ms. Medders' class. He began having problems with his schoolwork, and eventually he did not want to go to school.

The school counselor reviewed the situation and determined that Robbie had many of the signs of ADHD, together with impulsivity. Robbie was described as argumentative, rebellious, and defiant. Robbie's home history revealed none of the behaviors observed in school, so I asked Mrs. Snead to allow me to send questionnaires to Robbie's two previous teachers, as well as to a third teacher who taught him once a day for forty-five minutes. None of these teachers reported having a problem with Robbie.

Further evaluation revealed that the conflict between Mrs. Snead and Ms. Medders spilled over into the relationship between Ms. Medders and Robbie. When Robbie was able to change instructors, he thrived in his new classroom without any behavioral or attentional problems.

MENTAL HEALTH PROBLEMS

Several forms of mental illness can begin with symptoms of inattention, increased activity, and impulsivity. These include depression, childhood psychosis, oppositional defiant personality disorders, Tourette's syndrome, and autism spectrum disorders—all of which are discussed below. In addition, dissociative personality disorders, severe phobic reactions, and severe anxiety can also mimic ADHD.

Depression

Katilyn Rogers attended second grade at a public elementary school. Her teachers in first grade and kindergarten complained to her mother about a very short attention span and increased activity levels. Mr. and Mrs. Rogers sought the help of Dr. Seymour Luft, who requested that the parents and teachers fill out an ADHD questionnaire. According to this instrument, the child had ADHD in both the school and home environment. The doctor prescribed Ritalin.

After Katilyn had been on the medication for four weeks, Dr. Luft requested reports from her school and parents once again. These reports indicated that Katilyn was slightly less active, but her parents and teachers complained of her being sad and withdrawn. The physician doubled the dose of her medication. Mrs. Rogers called the doctor two days later, complaining that her daughter cried frequently for no apparent reason and further withdrew from her environment. Katilyn's medication was changed to Dexedrine, a stimulant used to increase alertness and decrease hyperactivity. The results were the same as with Ritalin.

At this point, Dr. Luft suggested that Katilyn be seen by one of my colleagues, a pediatric neurologist at a nearby medical school who specialized in neurobehavioral disorders. After an extensive examination and history aimed at all the potential causes of the child's symptoms, the neurologist made a diagnosis of depression. Interestingly, Mrs. Rogers had undergone psychiatric treatment for depression and took Prozac. Several relatives on the maternal side of the family also had a history of depression. After

Katilyn began treatment with appropriate antidepressant medication, her mood and school performance improved dramatically.

Depression in childhood appears more frequently than is usually realized. When children with sadness disorders are treated with stimulant medications, most of the time they do not improve and indeed their symptoms worsen. The late Dr. Warren Weinberg of the University of Texas Southwestern Medical Center and Dr. Roger Brumback, a Creighton University faculty member and editor of *Child Neurology*, have argued strongly that ADHD is a myth. In a study of 100 successive patients, Weinberg and Brumback concluded that in the majority of cases, what was called ADHD could be explained by various forms of depression, hypomania, learning problems, and disorders of vigilance in varying degrees.

I do not totally agree with their point of view. I believe that a primary neurological form of ADHD can run in families from one generation to another and can also, although less frequently, be caused by subtle insults to the brain. However, I agree with Weinberg and Brumback that depression in childhood is frequently overlooked. With the exception of the Vanderbilt form, which asks a few questions relating to depression and anxiety, the diagnostic questionnaires used most frequently by the educational and medical communities have asked questions related only to the *DSM*-IV criteria for ADHD. These instruments neglect to solicit information about the presence of various other problems and mental illness. In many instances, the diagnosis becomes a foregone conclusion and the real problem goes undetected.

Childhood Psychosis

Christian Dillon, a ten-year-old boy, was suspended from school for pushing a classmate. Previously, he attacked his teacher with a ruler. Christian never stayed in his seat, was always in motion, and seldom paid attention to what he was doing. At the urging of the school counselor, Christian's mother took him to a doctor, who had the school personnel fill out a brief form aimed at diagnosing ADHD. Based on this screen, the physician started Christian on Adderall. When the school saw little change in the child's behavior, the physician doubled the dose. Then the boy's behavior became bizarre. Christian began talking out loud in class to imaginary playmates, hid under his desk, shoved other children, and attacked the vice principal with a pair of scissors. Therefore, the school suspended him again. However, this time his mother requested testing for special education services.

A clinical psychologist conducted a series of tests. Upon interviewing the boy, the clinician found that Christian lived in a make-believe world of characters that he thought were real. The boy often saw others around him as enemies about to harm him. He heard voices in his head and felt that he possessed magical powers. A man riding on a black horse would tell him to hurt various other people or he would be punished.

Christian suffered from a form of childhood psychosis. Eventually treated with an atypical antipsychotic drug and psychotherapy, he showed considerable improvement. Symptoms of early childhood psychosis can easily be mistaken for ADHD if a proper and comprehensive evaluation is not done. Furthermore, many psychotic symptoms such as those Christian had can be made worse by the stimulant medications that are used to treat ADHD.

Oppositional Defiant Personality Disorders

Billy Norton did absolutely nothing his teacher asked. Nothing. Continuously demanding, he almost always required one-on-

one attention in the classroom. He rebelled against authority, bullied other kids, and demonstrated decreased alertness relative to classroom performance. Billy's activity level was extremely high, and he seldom finished assignments. Holding to any semblance of a schedule at home and at school was impossible.

At home, Billy fought constantly with his siblings, severely injuring his baby brother on one occasion. He refused to do household chores. Insisting on making a mess, he destroyed possessions belonging to others in the home. He lied and stole objects from other family members. He took many chances, such as playing with matches, and once set the living room curtains on fire.

Realizing the severity of the problem, Billy's parents sought the help of a physician who specialized in ADHD. The doctor believed in alternative therapies and not in the more traditional medical therapies. She did a skin test on Billy and told Mr. and Mrs. Norton that he had several allergies, particularly to food substances. Analysis of his hair, blood, and stool allegedly revealed vitamin and amino acid deficiencies. The doctor suggested that all of these problems caused the child's behavior.

Billy was placed on a diet devoid of milk, chocolate, nuts, and eggs. A high-potency mineral/vitamin regimen was begun, with natural supplements that contained much greater amounts of vitamins than in standard formulations. Ginkgo biloba and amino acids were added. In the six weeks after the start of this treatment, which the family adhered to religiously, Billy threatened a classmate with a knife, was expelled from school, stole thirty dollars from his grandmother's purse, and set a shed on fire. His decreased attention span, impulsivity, and other difficult behaviors in the classroom remained.

Eventually Billy's parents brought him to a child psychiatrist in our clinic, who diagnosed an oppositional defiant personality disorder with conduct components, and began psychotherapy and other forms of treatment. Currently Billy attends a special class for children with behavior problems, goes to two classes in a regular classroom, and no longer has problems with school personnel or classmates. Mr. and Mrs. Norton attended parenting classes. They applied techniques learned in these courses to Billy's behavior and have seen marked improvement.

Tourette's Syndrome

Another disorder that may be mistakenly diagnosed as ADHD is Tourette's syndrome, which in the early stages consists only of the inability to pay attention. Eventually, a combination of vocal tics (various guttural sounds, humming noises, or other unusual sounds) and motor tics (sudden twists, turns, blinking of the eyes, wiggling of the nose, and jerking of various part of the body) occurs. According to the *Diagnostic and Statistical Manual* IV, a diagnosis of Tourette's syndrome may be made when there is a combination of motor and vocal tics in a child. Some teachers interpret vocal tics as talking out loud, and thus a sign of impulsivity. Others mistake subtle motor tics as signs of overactivity. In some children the tics may be accompanied by animal sounds, cursing, and sudden outbursts of vulgarity in later stages. These behaviors, called coprophilia, do not have to be present to make a diagnosis of Tourette's syndrome.

Stimulant medications used for treating ADHD frequently make this malady worse by severely accentuating both the motor and vocal tics eventually observed in patients with Tourette's syndrome.

Autism Spectrum Disorders

Autism spectrum disorders include autism (higher and lower functioning), Asperger's syndrome, and Pervasive Developmental Disorder.

Ashley Cooper, a four-year-old who lived in a small town in north Texas, would frequently run about her house in a disorganized fashion, flitting from one place to another. She had delayed language and communication development. Having poor skills in social interaction, Ashley usually ignored other children and played in parallel isolation. On rare occasions she would rock and flap her hands when she was excited or upset. She began school at four, but paid little attention to the teacher's requests. Frequently she mimicked what her teacher said, but rarely gave independent answers.

Ashley's mother noted that she might approach strangers but would run screaming into another room when family members visited. Ashley pushed and shoved other children. Not knowing how to react to them when playing games, she eventually became frustrated and responded with acting out behaviors that were impossible to correct. Mrs. Cooper also noted that Ashley reacted strangely to loud noise, often covering her ears and going into a frenzy.

Alarmed by Ashley's inattentiveness and impulsive behavior, her teacher asked her mother to see a local doctor to determine if anything could be done. The child was started on stimulant medication, which only made the behaviors worse.

In the course of the workup, the school diagnostician suggested that Ashley had Pervasive Developmental Disorder, a condition similar to autism. Ashley was referred to a nearby developmental center for further workup. This was followed by treatment for Pervasive Developmental Disorder, which proved successful in Ashley's case.

INSTABILITY AT HOME
Illness and Death

Illness in a close family member may cause a child to act as though he has ADHD. Eric Montoya, a five-year-old, had been diagnosed with ADHD on a McCarney home and school scale, a questionnaire frequently used by school counselors for that purpose. His physician started him on Ritalin, eventually increasing the dosage. When Eric did not respond, the physician changed to Adderall and then Cylert (another medication used to treat ADHD) with an equal lack of success.

Eric's doctor eventually referred him to a pediatrician who specialized in developmental and behavioral pediatrics. A careful family history revealed that Mrs. Montoya had severe diabetes. On three occasions in the past year she had been hospitalized for cardiac failure and kidney problems. Currently she went for dialysis three times a week.

Any young child would find it hard to concentrate in school when he fears his mother is about to die. When children face the death of a close relative, they can benefit from several approaches.

- Support from the extended family is extremely helpful in this situation.
- Counseling and reassurance can provide support.

- In the event of the death of a close family member, some hospitals and clinics have cluster groups of children with similar problems and attempt to assist the children as they work their way through this difficult time.

Frequent Moves

Seventeen percent of the U.S. population moves every year. Typical movers are adults ages twenty-five to forty-four, with one to two children. Just the thought of a move, even within the same town or community, can cause great anxiety for children. The loss of friends, the change of neighborhood, and going to a new, unfamiliar school can translate into classroom and other problems.

T. J. Johnson's mother separated from his father and moved across town, taking T. J. with her. There the boy began a new school and did not get along with his classmates, had trouble paying attention to his teachers, and began fighting with his peers. Three months later, T. J.' s mother decided to move again, into a larger apartment. Once more this involved a change in schools. The new school's teaching methods were completely different, and T. J. struggled. In another two months his mother changed locations again. In the third school, T. J. had a complete collapse of academic performance and severe attentional and behavioral problems.

Divorce, Fighting, and Substance Abuse

Incessant fighting, separation, divorce, drug abuse, and drinking within the family can obviously cause distress that can lead to academic, social, and alertness problems in school, at play, and at home for children. Furthermore, because of the mobility of our society, links with extended family are frequently broken, leaving a struggling family much on its own, without substantial backup.

When a mother and father are divorced, it is important for both parents to be involved and work together to benefit the child. Children should maintain frequent contact with the noncustodial parent under normal circumstances. If the noncustodial parent is guilty of ridicule, abuse, neglect, or drug or alcohol abuse, contact should be avoided, or maintained only under close supervision. Unfortunately, the necessary spirit of cooperation may not exist. All too frequently, children become pawns in the legal, financial, and emotional battles of the involved adults.

MEDICAL IMITATORS
Seizures

Sheila Duran, a child of a physician in a rural community, failed the third grade and repeated the year. In her second attempt, she still had academic problems. Sheila's teacher said that she learned only parts of lessons and seldom retained entire ideas and concepts. Her history in her home and school environments indicated that she frequently did not pay attention and stared out into space much of the time. She also had outbursts of temper, became impulsive, and sometimes wandered off.

After consulting with the teacher and the school's counselor and diagnostician, a doctor in the community started Sheila on stimulant medications, but her behavior did not change, even with increasing doses. Two different stimulant medications were tried, again without benefit. Upon the advice of other parents whose children had similar behaviors, Sheila's parents tried the

Feingold diet, which sought to eliminate salicylate ash foods and dyes from her diet. Sheila's behavior worsened.

The Durans finally consulted a pediatric neurologist at a nearby children's medical center. During the course of his examination, the specialist noted that the child would follow only parts of instructions. When he made her breathe in and out rapidly during the examination, Sheila would suddenly grimace and stare off into space.

An electroencephalogram (brain wave test) showed that Sheila had abnormal discharges of energy from the right temporal lobe (lower central side of the brain). These caused her to experience partial complex seizures, which resulted in spells of decreased alertness and abnormal behaviors seen at home and in school. By not being fully conscious for brief intervals several times during the day, Sheila continuously lost bits of information related to her lessons and appeared inattentive.

Behavior outbursts, impulsivity, and wandering off may occur with this type of seizure pattern. These changes may be subtle and therefore more difficult to detect than the more common seizures that occur as jerking contractions of the limbs, incontinence, and loss of consciousness. Treated with appropriate medications, Sheila improved at home and school. She is now working on a master's degree.

Another type of seizure disorder that we observe in our clinical practice is called the absence or petit mal seizure. Children with this kind of seizure can have blinking of the eyes and loss of consciousness for several seconds as many as two to three hundred times a day.

Imagine yourself as a student in a classroom with a teacher giving a history lesson: "Christopher Columbus, from Italy, left . . . and discovered America . . . in 1965." If you had an absence seizure disorder and periodically missed components of the lesson every few seconds, you could easily come away thinking Christopher Columbus sailed from Italy (not Spain) and discovered America in 1965, not 1492. Multiply that by two or three hundred times a day and you can see how devastating this problem really is. The signs of the disorder are very subtle and can often be confused with disorders of learning and attention.

Lead Poisoning and Anemia

One of my patients, Whitney Smith, was the daughter of a postal worker and lived in an older section of Fort Worth in a house constructed in 1937. Her school performance was dismal, she caused disturbances in class with impulsive and rebellious behavior, and she lacked alertness. Testing by the school psychologist put her intellect in the borderline normal range, and her achievement scores were at a similar level. Inasmuch as she lived in a house built before 1965, my nurse drew a blood sample and sent it off to the laboratory. The results indicated that the lead level in Whitney's blood was moderately elevated and that she had severe iron deficiency anemia. When these problems were properly treated medically and from a public health standpoint, the child did better. Her behavior and academics both improved.

Another family brought baby Maria, fifteen months of age, to our clinic because she was developing at a significantly slower rate than other infants her age. Maria lived in a house constructed in the early 1960s. When I took a family history, I discovered that her two brothers, ages nine and eleven, had learning disabilities and ADHD. This family had resided in their home for thirteen years. Maria's blood lead level was significantly elevated. She was treated immediately and their house environmentally corrected by our local public health agency.

Blood lead levels for both of her brothers were in the mildly abnormal range. One can only guess the lead levels were considerably higher when they were younger. Tragically, even though they lived in older housing, none of these children had been previously tested for lead intoxication.

A new method called magnetic resonance spectrography can detect certain chemical changes inside the brain. This testing shows that even children with relatively low levels of lead intoxication exhibit a decrease in important brain chemicals and the loss of brain cells.

Children with school or behavioral problems should be tested for lead intoxication and anemia if any of the following circumstances are present:

- They live in housing that predates 1965.
- A parent works with heavy metals (for example, is a welder or works with car batteries).
- They live near smelters or in an area identified with lead pollution.

Some children live in environments that may be devoid of appropriate dietary levels of iron and other minerals. Their evaluation should include tests for anemia. Clinicians should explore family histories of blood disorders such as sickle-cell anemia (blood cells that are oddly shaped, cannot carry enough iron, and lack normal survival time) and thalassemia (abnormal formation of part of the red blood cells, resulting in their early destruction). Sickle-cell anemia occurs more frequently in people of African, Caribbean,

Guyanese, Panamanian, and Brazilian ancestry than it does in the general population. Thalassemia occurs in greater incidence in people with a Mediterranean or Southeast Asian background. Studies several years ago by Frank Oski, a pediatric hematologist, showed that severely anemic children can display inattention, increased activity levels, and diminished overall intelligence until the anemia is remediated. More recently, an article in *Pediatrics* concluded that children and adolescents with iron deficiency anemia had decreased achievement in school.

Medications

Medications used to treat a variety of disorders can cause symptoms that simulate ADHD. For, example antihistamines by themselves or in combination with a variety of drying agents, such as ephedrine (used to treat allergies), can make children very sleepy and thus inattentive, or cause them to be overactive. Treatment of asthma with Ventolin (an antiwheezing medicine) in oral or inhaled form can increase activity levels and make children appear jumpy. Phenobarbital, carbamazepine (Tegretol), valproic acid (Depakene), or other medications used for control of seizures can induce hyperactive behavior or cause extreme drowsiness. Medications such as Haldol, Thorazine, Mellaril, Zypraxa, Respiradol, and other antipsychotic medications used to treat a variety of medical and mental illnesses can cause somnolence or increase activity levels.

Allergies

Do allergies cause ADHD? That's what the lay literature frequently says. However, this occurs only rarely. Although a great many children have asthma, a runny nose, congestion, or sinusitis on an allergic basis, there is no greater incidence of ADHD in this population than in the public at large. Untreated or inappropriately treated nasal or pulmonary allergy can certainly cause a child to be irritable or less alert. Indeed, as pointed out previously, some of the medications used for treatment of various allergic conditions certainly can mimic symptoms of ADHD. Poor control of allergic symptoms can cause inattention and restlessness. In such cases, however, these traits are not linked to the central nervous system; they simply represent a child not feeling well.

Chronic Diseases

Children with any chronic disease or disorder can appear anxious, irritable, and not alert. Theo Poulos had severe, inoperable, congenital heart disease. When Theo was an infant, his doctors told his parents that he would not live beyond his first or second birthday. Despite his cardiologist's pessimistic outlook, he celebrated his eighth birthday, but in fragile health. Inasmuch as his cardiac problems could not be cured by an operation, he developed high blood pressure in his lungs. His skin turned a pale blue, and he had difficulty playing with other children without becoming short of breath.

In his first two years of school, Theo's grades were adequate relative to his overall intellect. A few weeks after he began third grade, however, his teacher called Theo's parents. "Theo won't pay attention to anything. He keeps talking in class and disturbs other children. I think you need to take him to his doctor and see if he has ADHD."

Theo's mother brought him to our clinic. I had know him most of his life. Theo felt comfortable with me and spoke freely. He revealed that he felt poorly every day, was exhausted, and couldn't concentrate. In addition, he feared he would die at any moment. I tried to reassure Theo as best I could and referred him to a sympathetic counselor.

Eventually, with new advances in cardiac surgery techniques, Theo's heart was repaired so that he could lead a more functional life. At no time did Theo actually have ADHD. Theo eventually finished high school and studied at a community college. A few months ago at a clinic where I consulted, he stopped me in the hall and showed me his new baby, who was being seen by one of the general pediatricians.

Endocrine Disorders

In 1993, *The New England Journal of Medicine* reported symptoms similar to ADHD in a group of patients with thyroid disease. Thyroid or other endocrine gland problems can certainly cause symptoms that simulate ADHD. In addition, severe hypothyroidism (low thyroid function) in infancy can cause mental retardation. Fortunately, many states now test for congenital hypothyroidism as part of a group of tests done on babies shortly after they are born. If laboratory tests indicate an inactive thyroid gland, such babies are easily treated early with replacement medication.

When a family history of a thyroid disorder is present or if a child presents symptoms of hyperthyroidism (an overactive thyroid gland) or hypothyroidism (an underactive thyroid gland), tests should be ordered to rule out these maladies. While studies from 1995 to 1997 concluded that routine screening for thyroid function in ADHD is unnecessary, one of my patients was a little girl with a history that suggested thyroiditis, a disorder in which the body's own cells attack the thyroid gland and make it enlarge.

After appropriate testing and a referral to a pediatric endocrinologist, the child was put on medication to ameliorate her symptoms.

Genetic Syndromes

Various genetic abnormalities can present symptoms that duplicate behavior patterns in ADHD. If a child has classic signs of Down's syndrome, the cause may be obvious. However, other congenital and genetic disorders may occur with less obvious clinical characteristics.

For example, fragile X syndrome, which frequently causes mental retardation in males, may appear as learning disabilities or as symptoms similar to those of ADHD. Only 50 percent of fragile X children have the telltale signs of the disorder, such as elongated faces and large, unusual ears. In the most severe cases, these children may display autistic symptoms.

One in 259 women is a carrier of the fragile X disorder. The full-blown genetic disorder occurs in one in 2,000 males. Seventy percent of the female carriers will have no signs of the genetic malady.

James Cole, a six-year-old, was brought to a developmental center after being diagnosed with a learning disability by his school and with ADHD by a pediatric neurologist. Examining him at the center, a clinician noticed his large, unusually shaped ears, his long face, and the wide spaces between his eyes. She ordered genetic chromosome testing, including special molecular gene testing for fragile X syndrome.

When the tests came back positive, additional molecular laboratory work was ordered to determine the severity of the problem. On the basis of this investigation, it was discovered that

James had a moderately severe disorder. Laboratory tests of family members indicated his sister and mother were both carriers of the disorder, although neither had any overt signs or symptoms.

Neurodegenerative Disorders

Other medical conditions that duplicate ADHD include neurodegenerative disorders, in which the child gradually loses function, development, and attention span. Additional imitators are neurological disorders such as chorea, in which the child seems to be in continuous motion.

Substance Abuse

Randy Charmichael was a twelve-year-old who had minimal problems with school and slight problems with alertness and behavior since the age of five years. However, he passed all his subjects with low C's and seldom had unsatisfactory behavior.

Shortly after the beginning of sixth grade, Randy stopped completing most of his work, slept in class a great deal, and began to fail each subject. His teachers suggested that he had ADHD and urged Randy's family to take him to a physician to evaluate him for medication.

The young man's pediatrician, after taking a detailed history, decided to do a drug screen, which indicated that marijuana was in his system. Unfortunately, drugs, particularly marijuana, are readily available in or near most schools, including private schools. Children who use drugs are frequently in a dream world of their own and cannot perform with any degree of alertness in a classroom.

Any young person twelve years of age or beyond who has been performing adequately and suddenly becomes very inattentive should be evaluated with a drug screen. In spite of what a parent may think or tell a clinician, many teenagers (and even younger children) take drugs. Most do not confide in their parents about these activities.

Sleep Disturbances

Maria Leva, eight years old, was seen by her family physician for problems with paying attention, impulsivity, and hyperactivity at school. She was prescribed stimulant medication without success. Her mother, on the advice of another clinician and friends, started her on the Feingold diet and eventually therapy with high-dose colloidal vitamins and amino acids. The child's problem continued.

After nine months of various therapies, Mrs. Leva consulted a developmental facility. She related to the clinician at the center that her child's private parochial school gave Maria four to five hours of homework a night, and that the child seldom went to bed before eleven. Mrs. Leva, a single mother who worked at a large airport, had to report to work at six in the morning. She awakened Maria between forty-thirty and five every morning to deliver her to her grandmother, who would take the child to school. Maria did not go back to sleep before the start of school. Inasmuch as this seemed to be an inordinate amount of homework, the child's doctor instructed Mrs. Leva to discuss the problem with the school's principal. This led to a reduction in homework so that the child could go to sleep by eight-thirty. With this plan in place, Maria's symptoms soon disappeared. She paid better attention to her class work and behaved in a normal manner.

Most parents have observed overtired children at their home. Frequently, they become overactive, develop crankiness, act out impulsively, and are not alert. Sleep disorders of various kinds can simulate the symptoms of ADHD. Some problems are situational, as with Maria. Other children have trouble falling asleep for reasons such as phobias (unrealistic fears), and yet others may awaken frequently during the evening and not be able to fall back to sleep. Most of these problems are easily controlled by adjusting sleep scheduling or with various mild medications.

In the past three years increasing numbers of parents have brought children from ages two to four to our center with what they perceive as abnormal symptoms of hyperactivity, impulsivity, and inattention. These behaviors are present in this age group under normal circumstances. Children between two and three have attention spans measured in minutes, are frequently in motion, and impulsivity is yet to be entirely controlled. A three-year-old being read to has an average attention span of about ten minutes.

These children fall into three categories. In the first group are parents who are intolerant of behavior normal for this age and want a medical fix with stimulants or other medications. The second rubric includes children who do not go to sleep until the late evening or beyond, and truly have abnormal behavior patterns as a result. When parents of these children are taught parenting skills and the sleep pattern is initially adjusted with small doses of a mild antihistamine such as Benadryl, the children's behaviors become age appropriate. Usually within a short period of time the medication used for sleep can be stopped. In the last category is a relatively small number of children who truly have abnormal conditions such as oppositional defiant personality disorders, autism spectrum disorders, or mental retardation.

In 2002 a study of more than a thousand children conducted by the University of Michigan showed an additional cluster of children with inattention, hyperactivity, and daytime sleepiness. These children had a condition called sleep-disordered breathing (SDB). Some characteristics of this disorder are snoring loudly more than half the time, short intervals of not breathing when asleep, and difficulty waking up in the morning. The researchers stated that excessive daytime sleepiness in these children was linked to inattention and hyperactivity. This association between snoring and behavior seems to be stronger in younger children, who have larger tonsils and adenoids and less breathing space in the area over their breathing tube. When doctors treat sleep-disordered breathing, the sleepiness leading to overactivity and decreased alertness is usually improved.

RULING OUT THE IMITATORS

An old saying goes that if something looks like a duck, quacks like a duck, and walks like a duck, it must be a duck. However, in the world of childhood disorders, if it looks like ADHD and acts like ADHD, it very well may be something else.

It is imperative that every child who appears to have clinical signs of ADHD undergo a complete evaluation that includes a comprehensive and careful history from all of the child's environments and employs good interviewing techniques with the parent, teacher, and child. A complete physical; a neurological exam testing reflexes, balance, and coordination; and a neuromaturational exam looking for progressive signs of maturation of the nervous system along a continuum should be performed. Clinicians can order appropriate laboratory and other diagnostic studies when indicated. Testing for learning problems is essential for every child who experiences academic problems.

ADHD: The Great Misdiagnosis

Needless to say, such an approach frequently necessitates the cooperation and interaction of professionals from several backgrounds. People in such endeavors should set up appropriate lines of communication to benefit the children involved and establish the maximum benefit of interlocking medical, educational, and psychosocial follow-up.

FIVE

Marketing the Great Epidemic

Several years ago a salesperson called me to inquire whether I needed a water filtration and purification system for my home. I promptly informed him that I had relied on the local water system for more than twenty years and had survived very nicely, thank you.

"If I can just come to your home and demonstrate our appliance, I can really convince you that you need a water purification system," he said. "Besides, I get twenty-five dollars for each demonstration and I need the money for my family."

"What the hell. Come on over and I'll take a look at it," I replied.

One week later he arrived at my doorstep with a large suitcase in hand. In my kitchen, he removed quite an array of glassware, filters, chemicals, a microscope, and other gadgets.

"Do you realize your water is full of minerals, germs, poisons, and impurities?" he began his sales pitch.

The young man promptly did an experiment using some of his chemicals and water from my kitchen tap. Almost immediately, a large amount of sediment appeared in the water. Using several other materials that turned the water an array of colors he claimed to identify several other harmful impurities in my city's water supply. Finally he pulled out his microscope and put a drop of water beneath the lens. "Look here at these little suckers, Doc."

I peered down at a harmless array of small organisms that peacefully coexist with humans.

The salesman nodded. "Pretty bad, isn't it? When your family drinks this crud, they can get sick awful fast."

No novice at the sales wars, I smiled and pointed out that no member of my family had gotten sick up to this point, and that actually our local water supply was better than four times the Environmental Protection Agency standards.

A strong sales pitch attempted to prey on all my emotions, from guilt if I did not provide the best for my family, to the terrible harm that would befall me personally if I did not adhere to the salesman's suggestions.

I thanked the young man and informed him that I would call him back if I became more interested. He packed his assorted property back into his carrying case and left, twenty-five dollars richer for his venture but without a sale.

Whatever does this have to do with ADHD? Many of the techniques this salesman used to sell his product are similar to the sales pitches used by those who market ADHD as a disorder and distribute merchandise, services, and medication to this population of more than eight million children and young adults.

A few of these tactics are:

- Identify a sufficiently large target population.
- Create a perceived or exaggerated need.
- Play on the fear of the unknown.

- Take advantage of parental feelings of guilt if a particular method, product, or remediation is not used.
- Declare that other forms of treatment or help are dangerous or unproven over time, or have serious side effects.
- Use a gimmick that makes a given product or methodology distinct from others.

Although the symptom complex of ADHD had been around for a very long time under other labels, the intensity of radio, television, and print media coverage reached a climax only after the malady was named ADD by the American Psychiatric Association. This intense coverage, although well intentioned and informative, nonetheless frequently made inaccurate and exaggerated statements.

Journalists reported lists of symptoms without warning that these might approximate normal variants in some children when occurring in lesser intensity, and that those traits should only be considered abnormal if they were severe enough to cause academic failure or significant problems with interpersonal relationships. Nor did the media point out that the same behaviors could occur in a plethora of other nonrelated disorders.

The author of one magazine for occupational therapists claimed, "One big clue to its existence in adulthood is an inner feeling on the part of the individual with ADHD that there is something not quite right." Many things may cause one to feel "not quite right," not just ADHD.

It became common for patients to say, "Oh, I see some of these traits in me and my child. I wonder if he or I have a problem. Maybe we ought to get evaluated." Unfortunately, this kind of thinking fanned the epidemic and among other things, led to an array of ADD psychiatric, psychological, and medical clinics and institutes dedicated to treating the new disorder. While some of these clinics functioned well, there were some problems. If a facility is aimed at a particular entity, a bias may develop toward making that the diagnosis. Other possible causes are overlooked.

At the height of this epidemic of misdiagnosis, many calls to our facility began, "My child's counselor in school says my child has Attention Deficit Disorder and I should get an ADD doctor." My standard response was twofold. "First, we should not put any label on the child without a thorough workup because we really don't know what the child has. Second, I work in the field of developmental behavioral pediatrics, and Attention Deficit Hyperactivity Disorder is just one of a great many disorders that I treat."

Entrepreneurism frequently overcomes logic. The great ADHD epidemic is no exception. People who sell high-dose vitamin products, for example, use the fear factor. They state that stimulant medications such as Ritalin are dangerous and there are no long-term studies about the effects of this group of medications. In truth, the stimulants have been in use for more than forty years. By the late 1970s more than 700 studies had examined the short- and long-term effects of medication related to the symptom complex we now call ADHD. As of today, scientists have probably conducted more than 1,000 investigations.

When these medications are used in proper doses for the appropriate disorder, they frequently produce dramatic benefits. Serious side effects usually occur when the wrong problem is diagnosed or medication is used in inappropriate amounts (Chapter 7, discusses medication). For those in this latter group, the consequences may be disastrous.

Some problems with ADHD medications have led to the formation of organizations such as Mothers Against Ritalin. This coalition has become a strong promoter of various alternative forms of therapy. A number of these groups, however, play on the fear that medical treatment for ADHD behaviors is dangerous.

The drug companies are not without fault. A national television program reported that a great deal of the funding for CHADD, a parent support organization, was from a company that manufactures stimulant medication. However, in all fairness, CHADD serves as an excellent support, advocacy, and educational forum. In 2002 the AAP published an ADHD Toolkit partly funded by McNeil Laboratories, the maker of a new, longer-lasting stimulant product.

One drug company that entered the stimulant medication market in 1996 best demonstrates the "you gotta have a gimmick" technique of entrepreneurism. At that time Richwood Pharmaceuticals bought the rights to a multiple-amphetamine-salt product called Obiterol, aimed at diet-conscious Americans. However, sales in that arena were not really going well. The corporation renamed the medication Adderall to coincide with the ADD epidemic, hoping that sales would increase. One physician with expertise in the field, from a developmental center in Seattle, believed that the manufacturer was overly aggressive in promoting its product and was quoted in the trade publication *Pediatric News* as saying, "This drug didn't do so well as an obesity treatment and now the company wants to cash in on a big treatment market."

The medication contained four different kinds of amphetamine salts that work at different time intervals. This medication differed somewhat from similar medications on the market and there were no generic versions of the product. This gave the manufacturer a distinct advantage.

The manufacturer approached medical professionals and sold itself as "your ADHD company." It printed information slips and data that promoted the disability and at the same time boosted its sales. Ciba used a similar tactic when it held the patent for Ritalin, as did Abbott with Cylert. Since 2001 almost all the new medications marketed for ADHD have followed a similar business formula, as well as directly marketing to the public.

However, with the exception of Dexedrine Spansules (see Chapter 7), which was less commonly used than Ritalin in 1996, there was no medication on the market that lasted throughout the school day and beyond. Therefore, the manufacturer of Adderall claimed that its product was long-acting (eight hours or longer) and that patients frequently needed only one dose a day to gain the desired outcome. It produced studies of more than 600 students, claiming that one-dose therapy worked much of the time. Richwood Pharmaceuticals literature noted that thirty-four children were not included in the study because they took doses of more than forty milligrams a day, indicating that a group of children required extra medication. A closer review of the treatment group revealed that approximately 65 percent of the children needed a second or third dose. In my own clinic, of 138 children who were prescribed Adderall, only eight are on this medication once a day.

Despite these contradictions to the pharmaceutical company's advertising claims, its salespeople and literature still touted the product as a long-acting medication. Eventually, Richwood stated that at times a second dose was indeed necessary, but not a third dose. While this drug in time became the second most popular medication used, it certainly does not meet the criteria for a once-a-day medication. In its haste to acquire market share, the manufacturer, now called Shire Richwood, sponsored studies targeting the more commonly used methylphenidates (such as Ritalin). Its researchers followed a flawed and biased protocol that used an insufficient dose of methylphenidate and compared it to normal doses of its multiple-amphetamine-salt product. Shire's advertising then claimed marked superiority to Ritalin. Eventually, some of its tactics came under the scrutiny of the U.S. Food and Drug Administration, which issued a letter accusing Shire Richwood of unsubstantiated comparative claims, including that Adderall was a longer-acting medicine than methylphenidate or other ADHD medications. The FDA ordered the drug company to immediately discontinue its advertising practices or face further action by the agency.

However, in the three years prior, this sales approach led to dramatic growth in the corporation, which in time was bought by a larger concern, Shire Pharmaceuticals. According to the manufacturer, prescriptions for this product rose from 200,000 in 1996 to over two million in 1998. Later that year, sales of Adderall eclipsed those of brand-name Ritalin, and by June 1999 reached 900,000 per quarter, though at that time generic Ritalin (methylphenidate) still held more than 60 percent of the market.

Another problem at that time was that the company told physicians to begin with half a tablet and gradually increase the dose, but did not give an end point. Aaron Kiley was one of several children I saw on referral who eventually wound up on massive doses of this "once-a-day" medication; in Aaron's case, it was three times a day. By the time we saw Aaron he was severely depressed and had hallucinations. Once his medical regimen was changed to a different drug at the appropriate dose for his size, he did well.

This sham finally came to an end in 2001, when Shire released its "new, long-acting" medication, Adderall XR (see Chapter 7) which truly lasts for nine hours or a bit beyond. Several salespeople, when confronted, stated that they really knew all along that shorter-acting Adderall was only a five- to six-hour medication. Many of these representatives deny advertising it otherwise. Currently, Adderall XR has a 26 percent market share, trailing only McNeil's Concerta, a long-acting methylphenidate product.

When children exhibit behavioral problems, their parents frequently become very frustrated and grab at any straw for help. All sorts of straws may come their way, from physicians, nutritionists, naturalists, inventors, and entrepreneurs. Some of these therapies come at great cost. Some do little or nothing for the child and at times even cause harm. Nonconventional therapies are addressed in Chapter 8. Parents should exercise caution when considering therapies and should make careful evaluations of available treatments.

SIX

Why Medical Treatments for ADHD?

In his book *The Myth of the ADD Child*, Thomas Armstrong, Ph.D., describes a little boy named Manny. The child struggled in school even with the aid of special education classes, psychotherapy, and counseling. The author states that although various forms of medication may have helped the boy, they would have changed his personality, altering his charm and uniqueness, "his Mannyness."

This brings to mind the case of a young teenager whom I treated for several years, Sarah Morton. Sarah was initially seen in our practice after another physician had diagnosed ADHD. After a thorough workup, we determined that many of her symptoms were based on a bipolar disorder—the sort of disorder marked by manic and depressive mood shifts. Her moods and self-deprecation became stable after we started her on antidepressant therapy.

When Sarah reached her fifteenth birthday, she abruptly decided that she no longer needed her medication because she "did not feel like her normal bubbly self."

Unfortunately, Sarah's usual bubbly self was accompanied by significant lows and thoughts of suicide. I cautioned Sarah and her mother that the decision could turn into a disaster. Nonetheless, Mrs. Morton fully supported her daughter's opinion, and Sarah stopped her medication.

Two months later, I received a call from a local emergency room. Sarah had swallowed a fruit salad of medication including Valium, Imipramine, Depakote, and Tylenol. The emergency service transferred her to the intensive care unit, and her survival was in doubt. Sarah hung on by a thread for a few days and then fortunately recovered. In time, she was placed in a psychiatric hospital until her mood disorder was stabilized on appropriate medication. Since then, she has stayed on her medication and has not attempted to kill herself.

Another patient at our clinic was Bubba Bartlett, a very impulsive child with ADHD and some other coexisting behaviors. Even though he caused severe disruptions at school, resulting in his suspension, his parents insisted on taking him off his medication because he was being "drugged." Bubba eventually burned down his home and injured a family member.

The lesson here is that most neurobiological disorders, such as depression and ADHD, are caused by abnormalities in either brain physiology, wiring, chemistry, anatomy, or a combination of these factors. The home situation and social interaction may modify or add to the problems that children with behavioral disorders manifest. However, the conditions involved are usually not solely a result of isolated and primary "psychosocial" problems.

We certainly would not avoid treating bacterial meningitis with an appropriate antibiotic and risk a dead or brain-injured child. We certainly would not fail to treat any serious seizure disorder with appropriate medication. No responsible clinician would refuse to give insulin to a juvenile diabetic; refusal would result in central nervous system problems, blindness, kidney failure, and even death. We certainly would not deny treatment to an individual who had an ailing heart, asthma, infected lungs, or cancer when medical therapy exists that can cure or control these maladies.

Neither should we refuse to treat true ADHD, in which a genetic or neurological condition underlies a child's dysfunctions in attention, activity cognition, executive function, and social interaction. Medical and behavioral studies indicate differences in how the brain is constructed and functions in ADHD children compared to others.

Some of the variations are revealed through magnetic resonance imaging (MRI), a technology that can actually duplicate the appearance of the inside of the human brain. At advanced research institutions, MRI machinery is so refined that one segment of the brain image can be sliced down to less than the width of a hair, enabling exact measurements of various areas.

MRI studies indicate that children meeting ADHD criteria have smaller right frontal lobes of the brain than other children. The front right part of their brains is smaller than or the same size as the front left part, the reverse of what is normally expected. Children with reading disorders show a similar pattern. Furthermore, the temporal lobes of the brain—the parts along the lower side of the brain—are equal in size, instead of disproportionate. Just beneath the thinking part of the brain are two small projections called the corpus callosum. This structure acts like a traffic cop, directing the signals that are on their way to the upper brain. The incoming signals must be directed toward only one particular side or area of the brain. If signals went to both sides of the brain at the same time, the result would be confusion.

ADHD: The Great Misdiagnosis

Studies indicate that in some children with ADHD, this anatomical traffic cop is smaller that what is considered normal. This size difference may affect the corpus callosum's control over how signals reach the thinking part of the brain. Other imaging studies at the National Institute of Health have shown that another area called the vermis, located in the cerebellum, a part of the brain that controls balance and motion, is smaller in kids with ADHD.

Research studies using radioactive tagged materials have examined blood flow to areas just beneath the thinking part of the brain. Children with ADHD have decreased blood flow in the areas that control motion, and an increase in flow in sensory motor areas. Symptoms related to heightened motor activity (hyperactivity) may be in part due to these differences in blood flow that exist in children with ADHD. The medications frequently used in treating ADHD reverse these blood flow patterns.

Tests of the body's use of sugar also indicate differences. When hyperactive adults were given a series of tasks, their glucose metabolism was significantly lower than is considered normal in certain front areas of the brain.

One might conclude that many of the behaviors seen in ADHD come from dysfunction in mechanisms contained in the front of the brain. Individuals who lose all or part of their frontal lobes will find it difficult to form a sequence of thoughts and therefore will have a great deal of trouble concentrating.

The front areas of the brain are involved in several functions. One is to keep us goal oriented and directed. The front part of the brain also helps us make appropriate responses to others without putting ourselves in harm's way, and to self-monitor so that we behave in a manner consistent with society's mores and demands. Another function is to help us with elaboration of thought and the ability to pull pieces of information stored in various other parts of the brain into focus when responding to a given situation. The front part of the brain also functions in abstract thinking, prognostication, and planning for the future.

Electrical charges in the brain have been studied by using a technology called computer-enhanced electroencephalography (CEEG). This procedure magnifies segments of a standard EEG many times over.

Two important electrical components of the brain are beta and theta waves. Theta waves are of much greater magnitude in younger children and during sleep. Beta waves may be thought of as the concentration or work-related reaction component. For example, when normal children do a reading task that requires concentration, the beta waves increase in relation to the theta. In children with ADHD or learning disabilities, the beta waves increase only insignificantly, and the ratio of theta to beta increases. This lack of an increase in beta activity during a task requiring concentration indicates a lack of activation of the brain electricity needed to create alertness during such an assignment.

When signals travel to various areas of the brain, they travel over wirelike structures called dendrites and axons. Between these wires are small gaps containing chemicals that tell an incoming message if it should progress forward or stop. These chemicals are called neurotransmitters. Two such substances, norepinephrine and its close cousin dopamine, help stop messages of no consequence from distracting a child from a more important task requiring concentration.

For example, if you are trying to concentrate on reading, you may need to screen out all sorts of messages coming into your body: the hum of an air conditioner, the persistent buzz of a computer, a fly on the wall, people walking outside the window, and the room temperature. If you lack or have low levels of norepinephrine or dopamine, chances are that you would become overly focused on all of those messages, which would come in with the same intensity. You therefore would not be able to concentrate on the task at hand.

These neurotransmitter substances have long been associated with attention deficit disorders. As a matter of fact, almost all the medicines effective in the treatment of these problems either increase the amount of these important chemicals in the central nervous system or prevent the body from getting rid of them.

From genetic or neurologically based ADHD to depression to schizophrenia, medications are now available that ameliorate symptoms. Either on their own or in combination with other therapies, medication can give people with brain disorders a more fulfilling, fruitful, and better life. In some instances a child's environment also needs to be manipulated or changed.

In 1987 I was lead author with Dr. Barry Russman, a pediatric neurologist at Newington Children's Hospital in Connecticut, of a statement on ADHD and medication that was written by the Committee on Children with Disabilities of the American Academy of Pediatrics. We set down a series of principles that should be adhered to when any clinician considers prescribing medication for children with disorders such as ADHD. These principles were reiterated when a revision of the statement was published in 1996, and have been quoted extensively in the medical literature, lay magazines, and books.

One key point of the statement is that medicine alone is not a panacea. Maximum benefit can be obtained when medication is used in combination with other approaches, such as appropriate educational remediation and modifications, behavior modification, and counseling for the parent and child. To neglect these other aspects of care is to put a bandage on a severely festering sore and then do nothing else. As a rule, the short-term gain is negated by severe long-term problems.

Another important issue is that physicians should not allow themselves to become surrogate prescribers for teachers, parents, or others who might advocate the use of medication even when there is no clear indication for medical intervention.

Before any decision is made to prescribe medication, provisions for the following should be in place:

- Quantitative identification of the exact problems causing the child difficulty in the home, school, play, and work environments.
- A working differential diagnosis to help rule out various other phenomena that can simulate ADHD or exist together with it. ADHD may not be a single disorder, but rather a common pathway for the expression of several different disorders or variants.
- Identification of coexisting problems in areas such as learning and maladaptive behavior disorders.
- Adequate follow-up of any medical treatment or other remedial programs on both a general and a quantitative basis.

In some instances, children placed on medication are not seen by their doctor for six months, a year, or longer. Medication without appropriate measurements and clinical tracking is inappropriate. Physicians who do not adequately follow these children are remiss in their duty to their patients. Without this kind of follow-up, a clinician has no awareness of when to increase medication, no idea if a child is succeeding over a significant period of time so that medications can be weaned, and no indication of whether other kinds of medication, therapies, or remediation are needed together with or instead of the initial choice.

After beginning medication, a child should be seen at intervals of four to six weeks. When a stable dose has been achieved, the time between visits may be extended to about three months. If a child has done well for several consecutive three-to-four-month intervals, a cautious, gradual weaning of medication may be attempted. If a child does poorly, increased dosages, changes of medication, or different combinations of medication should be attempted, and the child should be followed at closer intervals. In addition, the diagnosis should be reevaluated and the child's environment should be modified.

While genetic and neurologically based ADHD is a lifelong condition, the medication is seldom needed for the duration of a person's existence. Within my practice, approximately 40 percent of children are off medication by the beginning of middle school, and another 20 percent by the beginning of high school.

This decreasing need occurs for a variety of reasons. For one thing, humans are adaptive organisms. They frequently have the ability to use alternative neurobiological pathways and thereby compensate for various problems. Any good adaptive learning program incorporates alternative ways of performing tasks. These help children overcome and compensate for the various problems that occur with ADHD (see Chapter 9).

Furthermore, as a child progresses though the life cycle, particularly in the school environment, many more choices can be made academically and vocationally. Children have opportunities for greater mobility when they reach high school. In grade school, in contrast, children must sit at their desks like little soldiers and raise their hands even to ask to go to the restroom.

Adults can choose occupations that fit their learning and activity styles. When I practiced general pediatrics, I rarely had the luxury of staying in one place for very long in my office. My job required a great deal of movement, going from one examining room to another as I saw patients. One of my patients was extremely active throughout his life, and because he was constantly on the move, rarely took breaks. He channeled his enormous energy into work, and he became one of the youngest managers of a major retail chain.

Lastly, some youngsters mature at a slower rate than others. Some suggestion of this is present in the old ADD-R designation, which recognized that children with hyperactivity-impulsivity problems seemed to lose that component of their difficulty in their teen years. But central nervous system maturation may not be completed until the twenty-fourth year or beyond. Just as some boys do not develop facial hair until much later than others, and some girls may not begin menstruating until significantly after the norm, some young people may need more time for their nervous systems to mature.

After World War II, many veterans who had experienced great difficulty with alertness and learning in high school found that they could succeed at the university level. More recently, one of my colleagues in an associated field told me that he barely passed grade school and high school because he had great problems paying attention. He quit school, but eventually got a general equivalency diploma (GED). Years later he matriculated at a major university and ultimately obtained a graduate degree. His story is not uncommon.

SEVEN

Traditional Medical Treatments

Many medications are used to treat ADHD and related problems. Among them are the methylphenidate derivatives Ritalin, Focalin, Concerta, Ritalin LA, and Metadate CD and the amphetamine-related drugs Adderall, Adderall XR, and Dexedrine. These are classified as stimulant medications. Certain antidepressants, such as Strattera, Tofranil, and Wellbutrin are also used to treat the disorder.

The current era of medical treatment for children who exhibit symptoms of attention deficit and hyperactivity began more than sixty years ago. In 1937 a physician in Portland, Oregon, Charles Bradley, published a report claiming that more than thirty children he treated for hyperactivity, lack of attention span, and learning difficulties benefited from a stimulant drug called Benzedrine. This drug contained both the right and left sides of the amphetamine molecule, levo- and dextroamphetamine, which were mirror images of each other. Over the next twenty years Bradley published several case studies indicating that children with overactivity, decreased alertness, and academic problems improved on Benzedrine. However, there were a great many side effects due to the presence of levoamphetamine.

ADHD: The Great Misdiagnosis

This information lay dormant for many years, and attempts to treat children with similar amphetamines rarely occurred. In the 1960s researchers discovered that by eliminating the levo part of the medication they could get a similar beneficial result without many of the side effects. This led to the development of Dexedrine. Soon thereafter Ritalin appeared on the market as a medication that also treated short attention span, impulsiveness, and hyperactivity, but had far fewer adverse effects than Benzedrine.

Not unlike today, in many communities the medications became a cure-all for everything and anything that seemed to resemble increased activity levels, poor academics, and decreased attention span. This in turn led to extensive overuse in some areas of the country.

In 1971 the *Washington Post* reported that in Omaha, Nebraska, an inordinate number of students were being placed on the medication at the drop of a hat and that school policy openly favored this. The problem was picked up by many other media outlets and became a national scandal, with articles such as "Pills for Learning" and "Drug Abuse—Just What the Doctor Ordered." The public outcry that evolved led to the diminished use of both Ritalin and Dexedrine for many years.

However, as with many things in life, the truth is at neither extreme and tends to fall somewhere in the middle. In reality, treatment with these medications, used at appropriate dose levels, results in increased alertness, decreased activity levels, and decreased impulsivity in 70 to 80 percent of the children properly diagnosed with attentional and related problems. When a child is treated with these medications, however, it is important to establish whether the medication is having an effect or whether other factors are at work, such as the self-fulfilling prophecies of people in the child's environment. One recent study indicated a short-term placebo effect in 18 percent of those given a pill that had no stimulant medication at all.

How powerful is the sense of suggestion? Several years ago, one of my patients was Maria Ross, the daughter of another physician. Her parents told me that Maria had a learning disability and needed a special school. The preliminary workup on Maria, however, did not seem adequate to me. Further examination by an educational diagnostician revealed nothing significantly wrong.

Maria had already begun attending a private school for learning disabled children. Not willing to disturb her schooling, Dr. and Mrs. Ross elected for their daughter to finish the semester there. After four and a half weeks, the child's teacher sent home a note stating that Maria had an attention span problem. The teacher added that all the children in the classroom were on stimulant medication and that undoubtedly this would help Maria's progress.

Consequently, we saw Maria in our clinic, but a careful and thorough evaluation determined that she had no sign of ADHD. Dr. Ross, however, was convinced that unless he gave his daughter something, the teacher would forever hound the child and family about attentional problems. Dr. Ross worked at a large local hospital that had its own pharmacy center, and he enlisted its aid. The pharmacist made a harmless starch pill with the exact dimensions and color of a five milligram Ritalin tablet.

Being extremely curious about the results of the ploy, I went along with the scheme and six weeks later sent a school progress form to the teacher, asking various questions about Maria's academic performance and overall behavior. The form included a scale to measure behaviors associated with ADHD in areas such as alertness, self-monitoring, social interaction, and activity levels.

Much to my surprise, the teacher's responses indicated marked improvement in Maria. The teacher also noted that most of her other pupils took a second Ritalin tablet around noon. She strongly suggested another dose of medication at midday in order to benefit Maria's work even more. Thus a starch tablet was added at noon, with the expected results.

The next school semester, Maria attended a regular school without the need for any special education services and without any medication. The last report I had of Maria confirmed that she is a normal, healthy young woman and is doing extremely well.

Several lessons are to be learned from Maria Ross's experience. For one thing, observations may be much more accurate if there is not a preconceived notion about what medication is supposed to do.

Furthermore, if a parent is faced with an instructor who insists that a child will do well only if that youngster is on medication, then that teacher's fantasy should be realized. For example, a parent may give something harmless, such as a chewable vitamin pill, in the morning so that the parent can say, "Yes, Johnny is on medication for his problem." If a placebo is not used in this situation, the child could face a self-fulfilling prophecy of doom and failure.

Lastly, medications should be given an adequate trial of about four to six weeks to see if they are working. Otherwise, various mitigating circumstances in the school and home environment occurring on a day-to-day basis may interfere with the ability to make proper clinical judgments.

Traditional Medical Treatments

Even though medications such as Ritalin or Dexedrine act rapidly, we may not be able to judge their optimal benefit or failure until a child has been taking the medication for several weeks. Certainly, if a serious side effect occurs, any trial of medication should be adjusted or terminated.

METHYLPHENIDATE DERIVATIVES: RITALIN, FOCALIN, RITALIN SR, CONCERTA, RITALIN LA, METADATE CD, CYLERT

Ritalin

Regular Ritalin is a short-acting form of dextrolevomethylphenidate and begins to work in thirty minutes. It usually peaks in two hours and its effectiveness is spent after four hours. This means that it must be given three times a day at four-hour intervals to work throughout the school day and into the late afternoon and early evening. Ritalin may be dosed in two ways. It may be given at regular doses of between 0.3 and 0.8 milligram per kilogram of the child's body weight. What this means is that if a child weighs forty-two pounds, or about twenty kilograms, a dose of 6 to 16 milligrams would be useful. Ritalin is manufactured in 5, 10, and 20 milligram doses. The maximum dose should never exceed 25 milligrams, three times a day.

Another method recently recommended by the APA is to begin with 2.5 or 5 milligrams a dose and then adjust the amount upward in small increments every two weeks until there is a relief of poor attention span, hyperactivity, and impulsivity, or side effects occur. The APA suggests not to exceed 60 milligrams a day. In small children below the age of five, 1.25 to 2.5 milligrams per dose is the starting point and doses should be increased very slowly.

Focalin

Focalin is a short-acting form of methylphenidate. Like amphetamines, methylphenidate is composed of two chemical parts, levomethylphenidate and dextromethylphenidate. They are mirror images of each other. Dextromethylphenidate treats ADHD by increasing attention span and decreasing hyperactivity and impulsivity. The levomethylphenidate half contributes little to the treatment aspects of the drug and causes many of the side effects. Therefore, the manufacturer engineered a drug that contains only the dextromethylphenidate. The result is a medication with beneficial effects on ADHD but without many of the side effects of other stimulant medication (discussed later in the chapter).

Focalin begins to work in thirty minutes and has an effect of about five hours. The amount of medication necessary to have a clinical effect is half that of regular Ritalin, and it often may be given twice a day. Focalin seems to be of most value when side effects of other medications for ADHD are severe and thus limit their use. It is also useful for dosing between three and five o'clock in the afternoon, when other stimulants given in the late afternoon may interfere with sleep. Focalin is currently being tested in a long-acting form, which should be available around 2005.

Ritalin SR

In the 1980s the manufacturer of Ritalin made its first attempt to produce a longer-acting product and called it Ritalin SR. The medication was encased in a wax matrix and released poorly over time. Studies have shown that Ritalin SR takes longer to have an effect and puts half as much medicine into the system as regular Ritalin.

A 1987 article in *Pediatrics*, the journal of the American Academy of Pediatrics, compared the results of both types of Ritalin on a group of children in a double-blind investigation, in which the professionals observing the children did not know which ones were receiving Ritalin, Ritalin SR, or no medication at all. On an array of rating scales that measure many different behaviors, the children on Ritalin SR did not show as much improvement as did those on regular Ritalin. In my own experience, this medication seems to have an effect for only five to six hours at most, and as confirmed by the researchers, does not help as much as the short-acting form. Furthermore, when the medication wore off, many of my patients experienced extreme problems with agitation and mood swings.

Concerta

When Concerta was approved by the FDA in 2000, it became the first true long-acting medication for the treatment of ADHD. The active ingredient of the medication is generic methylphenidate (Ritalin). The manufacturer of the product did not invent anything new, but used a technology called the OROS system, previously used in medication to treat asthma and urinary incontinence. This clever system utilizes a nondissolvable capsule. The outer part of the capsule is coated with regular methylphenidate (Ritalin) so that it begins to dissolve soon after the capsule is swallowed. It begins to have an effect in about thirty minutes. The inside of the capsule has a pastelike methylphenidate. A tiny hole is drilled with a laser on the top of the capsule. The bottom of the capsule contains a material called an expander. The walls of the capsule are designed so that they permit fluid to enter as the capsule passes through the intestinal tract. When the fluid is absorbed, the expander acts like a sponge and gradually enlarges, pushing out the methylphenidate above it in small metered amounts over twelve hours.

More than 400 children were given this medication or a looka-like capsule that contained no medication. This was done in a controlled classroom setting and at home. The children taking the Concerta did better than the children taking the capsule with no medication on measures of attention span, hyperactivity, impulsivity, and academics for twelve hours. Blood was drawn from some of the children and indicated a smooth distribution of the medication over the entire time interval, without significant peaks and valleys.

Since this medication lasts for twelve hours, it only requires one dose a day. A capsule taken at seven-thirty in the morning covers the entire day in the classroom, with enough medication still on board to help a child maintain sufficient concentration to complete homework (optimally between four to six p.m.). Most parents put their children to bed between eight-thirty and nine o'clock. This leaves approximately one hour without medication.

There are some disadvantages with the use of Concerta in younger children. If a child cannot swallow the capsule whole, it cannot be cut in half, mashed, or chewed. Doing any of these actions interferes with the integrity of the system and effectively destroys the time-release mechanism. Inasmuch as the capsule does not dissolve, this medication should not be used in children with a diagnosis of gastroesophageal reflux (GER), past diagnosis of or surgery for a narrowed feeding tube (pyloric stenosis), Crohn's disease, or any disorder of the intestines where the size of the intestines was surgically altered, or when a disease process interferes with absorption.

Since the Concerta outer capsule does not dissolve in the intestinal tract, it is not unusual to find it intact after elimination from the body.

Concerta comes in 18, 27, 36, and 54 milligram capsules. A child on 5 milligrams of short-acting Ritalin three times a day should begin on 18 milligrams of Concerta once in the morning; 10 milligrams of Ritalin three times a day equals 36 milligrams of Concerta once a day; 15 milligrams of Ritalin three times a day equals 54 milligrams of Concerta once a day. Young adults on 25 milligrams of Ritalin three times a day may be converted to 72 milligrams of Concerta (two 36 milligram capsules) once in the morning.

I begin patients who have never been on Ritalin before with the lowest dose, 18 milligrams a day, and increase every three weeks as necessary until symptoms improve. I never exceed 72 milligrams a day.

Ritalin LA

Ritalin LA was also studied in large groups of children, some of whom were given the medication and some a lookalike capsule. It was found to work quite well. It contains two sets of plastic-coated beads. As the capsule melts, the first set of beads is released and takes effect in about thirty minutes, the same as a regular short-acting Ritalin tablet. The plastic on the second set of beads is designed so that it does not dissolve and release medication until four hours later. Researchers have established the duration of action of this drug to be nine hours. Exactly 50 percent of the beads release immediately and 50 percent four hours later.

If a child cannot swallow the capsule, a parent can open it and sprinkle the contents on a teaspoon of applesauce followed by a glass of water. There is no difference between taking the capsule in this manner or as a whole capsule. This method of administration definitely has an advantage for young children and for those older children who cannot swallow a capsule or pill that must be ingested intact to be effective. This delivery system, called "sprinkles," has been used for many years to treat asthma and seizure disorders.

A nine-hour medication given at seven-thirty in the morning is spent by four-thirty in the afternoon. Therefore, it is not present to help the child pay attention for homework. In such situations it is helpful to use a short-acting stimulant with minimal side effects, such as Focalin, soon after school to cover the early evening gap.

Ritalin LA comes in 20, 30, and 40 milligram capsules. When treating children who have already been on stimulant medication, I begin with the equivalent total dose of regular Ritalin taken during school hours. For an example, a child on 10 milligrams three times a day takes 20 milligrams of medication during school. Therefore, she would begin on 20 milligrams of Ritalin LA once in the morning.

Metadate CD

Metadate CD uses generic methylphenidate enclosed in two different sets of plastic beads within a capsule. Thirty percent of the beads are immediately released so that the medicine has an initial effect similar to Ritalin LA and Concerta. The remaining 70 percent, contained in another set of beads, are defused through a membrane over the next eight hours. Studies show the duration of action of this medication to be in the eight-to-nine-hour range. Therefore, to be effective in the early evening for homework, Metadate CD must also be supplemented with a short-acting stimulant after school. It too may be used as a sprinkle when a child cannot swallow a capsule or pill.

Metadate CD comes in 20 milligram capsules. Conversion to Metadate CD for children on short-acting methylphenidate (Ritalin) is comparable to that of Ritalin LA. For a child not previously on a stimulant medication, doses should begin with the smallest amount (one 20 milligram capsule) and then slowly be increased to the point of reducing hyperactivity, inattention, and impulsivity. If this is not accomplished at the 60 milligram level (three capsules), the child should have a trial on another medication.

Cylert

Cylert (pemoline), another stimulant medication that has the same basic effect as Ritalin, requires three or four weeks before effectiveness can be determined. Cylert can be administered once in the morning. Unlike other stimulant medications, which need a special, regulated prescription pad in many states and must be filled within a specified time, Cylert may be prescribed on a regular prescription pad. However, Cylert is seldom used anymore because of significantly altered liver function in forty-four children. Since the drug was first used, thirteen children developed total liver failure, resulting in death or liver transplantation within four weeks of the first appearance of the problem. This represents a rate seventeen times that of the population at large. Before use, parents must sign a paper acknowledging their child is at risk for liver failure that could result in death and must comply with biweekly blood tests of liver function. Inasmuch as there are excellent medications with few serious side effects for the treatment of ADHD, this drug should never be used under any circumstances.

With any of the stimulant medications, if a little bit is good, a whole lot can become a rapid disaster.

Seven-year-old Jeffrey came from another state to live with his aunt, who resided near one of our offices. He was a troubled boy, with serious emotional problems stemming from brain abnormalities caused by parental drug and alcohol abuse. Jeffrey had been deserted by his mother, then abandoned by his father in a motel. Social services in his home state placed him in one foster home after another. However, his attentional problems, hyperactivity, impulsivity, acting out, rebelliousness, anger, and refusal to follow instructions prevented any permanent foster placement.

Jeffrey also had poor recollection of facts and sequences. He was extremely hyperactive, flying rather high. Another problem for Jeffrey was that he was considerably underweight.

When I reviewed Jeffrey's chart, I noted he was on 60 milligrams of Ritalin three times a day, a huge dose for his size. In addition, he had been on as much as 90 milligrams three times a day. Apparently, the clinicians seeing him had failed to grasp that other medications were available to treat his multiple problems. Instead, they just continued to increase Jeffery's Ritalin to a point beyond toxicity.

Giving methylphenidate (Ritalin) beyond a dose of 1 milligram per kilogram of body weight, or 0.5 milligram per kilogram for the amphetamine derivatives Dexedrine and Adderall, actually can lead to decreased memory and attention span. Dosing the new long-acting medications above recommended levels causes similar problems.

AMPHETAMINE DERIVATIVES: DEXEDRINE, ADDERALL, DEXEDRINE SPANSULES, ADDERALL XR

Dexedrine

Dexedrine is a short-acting medication that takes effect in one hour and lasts for more than five hours in most children. In a small percentage of patients the medication may last throughout the school day. It comes in tablet form in varying strengths. The dose for this medication is one-half that of Ritalin. By eliminating levoamphetamine from the formula, the manufacturers of this medication decreased many of the adverse effects seen with the early stimulant medication, Benzedrine.

Adderall

Adderall, another short-acting stimulant medication, contains four different amphetamine salts, including one of levoamphetamine. Although originally marketed as a long-acting drug by the manufacturer, in reality it seldom lasts more than five hours. In my clinic Adderall had an effect beyond six hours less than 20 percent of the time. More often two doses a day were necessary and in some children a third dose.

In 2000, researchers from the National Institute of Mental Health presented a paper at the annual meeting of the New Clinical Drug Evaluation Unit at Boca Raton, Florida, comparing Dexedrine and Adderall. They found virtually no difference in duration of action of the two drugs. Although not significant, afternoon hyperactivity ratings were actually better for Dexedrine than Adderall.

According to some clinicians, Adderall has a slightly smoother effect than Ritalin or Dexedrine. However, I have failed to see evidence of that in my practice.

Due to massive marketing efforts by the manufacturer, short-acting Adderall became the second most commonly prescribed medication for disorders of attention, overactivity, and impulsivity until Shire Pharmaceutical's new product, Adderall XR, a true long-acting form of the drug, was marketed in 2001.

A study by William Pelham and his associates, published in the journal *Pediatrics*, compared Adderall and Ritalin. This study indicated that Adderall required doses approximately one-half the amount of Ritalin, and thus similar to doses for Dexedrine. Adderall and Ritalin produced the same kind of behavioral changes.

Some of the manufacturer's literature and sales personnel suggested that Adderall could be used less frequently in the course of a day if the initial doses were given at a higher level than previously recommended. Pelham's group noted, however, that higher doses of Adderall did not cause incremental improvement. Furthermore, parents were less likely to continue the higher doses of Adderall. Shire Richwood also funded studies comparing Adderall and Ritalin, and claimed the superiority of Adderall based on their data. However, some of these studies were badly flawed or involved small numbers of children. The FDA reviewed all studies that compared Ritalin and Adderall and concluded that there was little or no difference in how the two medications affected children with ADHD.

Dexedrine Spansules

Dexedrine Spansules are composed of beads of medication that release at different times. The effect on children with ADHD is the same as with short-acting Dexedrine, but in many children the duration of action is eight hours. This was the first stimulant medication used as a sprinkle with small children who could not swallow a capsule.

Adderall XR

With the development and release of Adderall XR, Shire marketed its "true" long-acting medication, indicating that in reality it regarded Adderall as a shorter-acting medication.

Traditional Medical Treatments

Adderall XR is a polymer-plastic-coated bead application of multiple amphetamine salts, including three salts of dextroamphetamine and one of levoamphetamine. Several hundred children were given Adderall XR and a lookalike placebo. The medication was effective through nine hours of testing. The first set of beads enters the system soon after the capsule is swallowed and the second set is introduced after four hours. Inasmuch as Adderall can have an effect for five to six hours, the duration of this medication is more likely in the ten-hour range. The literature reports a somewhat higher side effect profile than the other new long-acting stimulants. Adderall XR comes in 5, 10, 15, 20, 25, and 30 milligram capsules.

One study indicated that Adderall XR is poorly absorbed from the intestinal tract when a child eats a high-fat-content breakfast before taking the capsule. Therefore, breakfasts consisting of fried eggs, bacon, potatoes, etc., should be avoided in children taking this medication.

SIDE EFFECTS OF
STIMULANT MEDICATIONS

On average, some of the problems associated with stimulant medications are greater with Dexedrine and multiple amphetamine salts (Adderall) than with the methylphenidates (Ritalin).

The two most common side effects with stimulant medications are loss of appetite and insomnia. It was feared for a time that a loss of appetite could result in diminished nutrition and growth. Studies of children who remained on these medications for several years reveal that their height is not significantly different from that of their peers; weight gain trails their counterparts, but not to a statistically significant degree. A 1991 study followed a group of children into adulthood and found no significant difference in height between them and nontreated individuals. In 1999 a study involving six institutions and over 600 children also failed to show any clinically significant differences in growth.

Sleep problems associated with stimulant medications appear to be transient in most children, if they occur at all. Among the newer long-acting medications they are seen most frequently with Concerta and Adderall, although the incidence with either of these medications is not overwhelming. They are least likely to occur with Focalin. If sleep disturbance persists, parents can administer a small dose of over-the-counter Benadryl, which works quite well and for the most part can be discontinued after a brief period of time. Melatonin (see Chapter 8) can also help to treat problems with sleep arising from stimulant use.

Sometimes children will complain of a headache or stomachache. It is not wise for a parent to ask a child if he has a hurting tummy or head, because many children become overresponsive to the question, suggestion, and attention. When a child does complain, see if the symptom disappears without further treatment. A statement like "it will be okay if you rest" might suffice. If the complaints are frequent and severe enough to require medication for relief, a change of medication might be needed.

Many children experience headaches and stomachaches long before the start of a medical regimen, and these should not preclude them from beginning treatment. Most of the time, neither the incidence nor intensity of these symptoms will change. Nevertheless, information about headaches and stomachaches should be ascertained before any physician writes a prescription for a stimulant or other medication.

A child behavior clinic in our city saw ten-year-old Sharon Roden. They made a diagnosis of ADHD, and Sharon began to take a small amount of Ritalin. When her mother noted that Sharon's eyes were blinking frequently, her mouth twitched, and her shoulders jerked with some regularity, she called the physician who placed her on the medication. He said that the child had Tourette's syndrome and that the drug should be stopped immediately. That was not true. Although Sharon had tics and jerks, she did not have a tic disorder such as Tourette's syndrome. Rather she was manifesting a rare side effect of Ritalin.

She was referred to me by one of my other patients. I stopped her Ritalin and started her on Focalin. Because Focalin does not contain levomethylphenidate, it does not cause tics as often as Ritalin. In past years, when a child was switched to Dexedrine, which does not contain levoamphetamine, many times the tic would disappear. Adderall does contain a levoamphetamine component and so should not be used as a substitute for Ritalin when tics occur. Twelve patients from our clinic who had tics with either Ritalin or Adderall were placed on Focalin. Only two of these continued to manifest tics; the other ten remained on Focalin without any difficulties.

When twelve-year-old Anna Finkelstein was placed on Ritalin, her inattention and hyperactivity improved significantly. However, her teacher and parents noted significant withdrawal and what they interpreted as depression. The dose was cut in half, but Anna still manifested the same problem. Her pediatrician, who had a good background in child behavior, searched further and found that Mrs. Finkelstein had a history of depression. After the medication was stopped, the pediatrician determined that Anna had a similar mood disorder. She was switched to appropriate antidepressant medicine and did well.

All stimulant drugs can cause withdrawal as a side effect when a dose is too great for the given individual. In that case the medication should be adjusted to a lower level. When a tendency to depression or symptoms of sadness are present, no matter how slight, the stimulants frequently make the problem worse. When there are coexisting symptoms in the same individual, it is important to gain control of the sadness disorder first. In some instances, this will suffice to control the entire problem. If the ADHD symptoms persist after the mood disorder lifts, a trial on stimulants may be successful.

Adderall XR causes mood lability and nervousness in more than 15 percent of children, according to the manufacturer's own study. In our own patients, this problem occurs almost 20 percent of the time. Furthermore, if aggression and irritability are a part of a bipolar disorder, these symptoms seem to worsen on that medication in many children.

Parents frequently ask if stimulant medications must be used after school and during holidays, summers, and weekends. Some parents like to interrupt the regimen for various reasons. For example, short-acting Ritalin, Dexedrine, and Adderall frequently cause problems with insomnia if used at four or five o'clock in the afternoon. Focalin is much less likely to cause insomnia when used in the afternoon. Among the long-acting medications, this problem is less likely to occur with Ritalin LA and Metadate CD, which are pretty well spent by the end of the school day.

In the past, when clinicians thought that stimulant drugs caused severe loss of weight and lack of growth, they recommended "drug holidays." They reasoned that this allowed a time-out during which children could resume their normal appetites and thus reestablish gains in height and weight. In our community a number of years ago, a lecturer suggested that, because

Traditional Medical Treatments

ADHD is a pervasive process, the medication should be used every day of the week, including holidays and summer vacations. Neither point of view is entirely correct. Any treatment plan should be tailored to a child's individual needs.

Mrs. Rivera was extremely concerned that nine-year-old José had no appetite when he took his medication. Therefore, without consulting her physician, she stopped the child's Adderall XR on weekends. José's behavior deteriorated. Refusing to do even the simplest chores, he challenged his mother's authority at every opportunity. José could not follow through on any task and became extremely overfocused on various disrupters in his environment. He frequently got into fights with siblings and children in the neighborhood. After three weeks, his doctor persuaded Mrs. Rivera to continue the child's medication on weekends.

On the other hand, when seven-year-old Jermain Larson was initially evaluated, his mother indicated that she had no problem controlling his inattentiveness with structure, redirection, and elimination of distracting factors after school and on weekends. Therefore, his pediatrician decided not to continue his medication during those times. Jermain remained on this regimen and did extremely well. Some children will have socially maladaptive, hyperactive, impulsive, and inattentive behavior not just in school, but afterwards and on weekends. They must continue on medication during these times. Children who do not exhibit behavioral problems, or whose environments can be sufficiently structured so that only minimal problems become evident, should obviously not be on stimulants outside of school.

In the rare event that a child is on Cylert, parents should know that this medication must be present in the blood at a steady level, and so needs to be taken every day.

There are times when stimulants should not be used, or used only with a great deal of caution. They should not be used by children or young adults with psychotic disorders, glaucoma, or hyperthyroidism, or if they are taking an MAO inhibitor for depression. They should be used cautiously if the child has a history of motor tics or anxiety, or if there is a family history of Tourette's syndrome or drug abuse. In children with cardiovascular disease these medications should never be used without the approval of a competent pediatric cardiologist. Over the years, several of my patients who had congenital heart disease took Ritalin with the approval of their cardiologist, and suffered no cardiac side effects.

ADDICTION AND ABUSE

One issue of frequent concern to many parents is addiction to Ritalin. This is an issue periodically raised by various groups and the media. Dr. Nora Volkow, chair of the medical department at Brookhaven National Laboratory, determined that Ritalin is absorbed by the brain more slowly than highly addictive drugs. Therefore, it does not cause the rapid high that drugs such as cocaine, amphetamines, or "ecstasy" initiate. This is probably why children taking Ritalin do not abuse it or develop addictions. Although the amphetamine derivatives are theoretically more addictive than Ritalin, I have only rarely seen abuse or addiction to Dexedrine or Adderall in my practice.

The new nonstimulant drug Strattera (atomoxetine) has no potential for addiction as it does not affect the part of the brain that causes that problem.

Another report indicates that when children with ADHD took appropriate medication for their disorder, they had no greater rate of substance abuse than the population at large. On the other hand, children who were untreated for their ADHD had a significantly greater incidence of substance abuse than their unaffected peers. Dr. James Cooper, at a 1998 National Institute of Health (NIH) ADHD conference, declared that research indicated low levels of Ritalin abuse among high school seniors: "From a public health perspective, our primary problems with stimulant abuse in the United States are with illicitly produced drugs such as cocaine, methamphetamine, and amphetamine." More recently, a U.S. General Accounting Office survey of high school principals also noted a minimal incidence of illicit sales of prescribed stimulant medications on their campuses.

Russell Barkley followed 147 children with ADHD for thirteen years. In January 2003 he reported in *Pediatrics* that by adulthood there was no evidence of increased substance experimentation, use, or abuse in this population.

THE ANTIDEPRESSANTS: TOFRANIL, NORPRAMINE, STRATTERA, WELLBUTRIN

When stimulant medications do not achieve the desired effect in treatment of ADHD, or if intolerable side effects occur, physicians frequently turn to antidepressants as a second tier of medications. Clinicians many times also use this second group of medications if the attention deficit is also associated with anxiety, mood disturbance, or depression.

Tofranil and Norpramine

Tofranil and Norpramine, both tricyclic antidepressants, were initially manufactured to treat only depression. They prevent the nervous system from breaking down the chemical norepinephe-rine and thus cause a buildup of this agent.

After a few years of observing the effect of these antidepres-sants, physicians noted that Tofranil and some others helped other conditions as well. First, they noticed that 60 percent of nocturnal bed wetters coincidentally improved when given Tofranil for their depression. Then physicians observed that when Tofranil was pre-scribed for depressed children with anxiety and attention deficits, these latter two symptoms also improved.

The next step was to try these antidepressants on children who had ADHD (in that era called MCD), but did not manifest symp-toms of depression. While not as effective as stimulant medica-tions for ADHD, Tofranil still helped the condition and became especially useful when the stimulants caused severe side effects or did not work. Tofranil also became a standard pediatric treatment for bed-wetting as well.

Norpramine (desipramine) was marketed after Tofranil and had an even more beneficial effect on ADHD symptoms. Unfor-tunately, six children died suddenly from cardiac causes while taking Norpramine. As a result, the drug is seldom used anymore. Dr. Diana Atkins, a pediatric cardiologist, reported at a 1999 meeting of the American Heart Association that three of these pa-tients, by history or at autopsy, were discovered to have previously underlying and undetected heart disease, which by itself could have caused their demise. It remains unclear if the three other children had a predisposing heart problem as well. However, Dr. Atkins said, "The history of when these children died is very different from what we see with drugs that we know have similar effects." She concluded that the risk of sudden cardiac death from the tricyclic antidepressants is quite low.

Traditional Medical Treatments

Following the Norpramine scare, however, clinicians began using Tofranil with extreme caution. The psychiatric community almost always obtains an electrocardiogram (EKG) to determine heart function and rhythm before prescribing this medication, and most psychiatrists repeat EKGs at intervals throughout the treatment process with tricylic antidepressants such as Tofranil. In a 1996 policy statement on ADHD and medication, the AAP said that no proof existed that such monitoring could help identify which children were at risk for a cardiac calamity, and that "routine electrocardiogram (EKG) monitoring is not indicated at this time." At least one other medical article stated that changes in the electricity of the heart only occur when the dose exceeds 2.5 milligrams per kilogram of body weight. That means that in a child weighing forty-two pounds, or twenty kilograms, significant changes do not occur until the dose reaches 50 milligrams of medication per day. Ultimately, the judgment of the physician treating children with these medications will determine the need for an EKG.

Children who have cardiac disease should not be started on the tricyclic antidepressants without a consultation with a knowledgeable pediatric cardiologist. In any case, it would seem prudent to use other forms of medication unless a distinct need is present. Parents should always be made aware of the facts concerning the tricyclics. They are part of the selection process and need to give informed consent whenever this type of medication is used.

Other significant side effects of the tricyclic antidepressants include abdominal pain and headache. Many children complain of sleepiness when first starting these mediations. Usually this dissipates after several days. If not, the dose should be adjusted downward.

The tricyclics take at least two to three weeks to begin to show any benefit. Any change prior to this time is probably a placebo effect.

This group of drugs works on a level basis. Therefore, even if weekends are not problematic, doses have to be given every day. During summers or holidays, the tricylics may be discontinued if there are no problems in the home environment without medication. However, these drugs should be restarted at least three weeks before school begins.

Strattera

In late 2002 Strattera (atomoxetine) became the first nonstimulant medication developed primarily to treat ADHD. Its manufacturer engineered a drug that potently inhibited the central nervous system from reabsorbing norepinephrine, thereby increasing its levels in the nervous system to foster better alertness and decrease activity levels. Unlike antidepressants such as Norpramine and Tofranil, Strattera was designed so that it did not interfere with the electrical impulses and rhythm of the heart.

More than 200 children were given trials on Strattera and a placebo. There was significant relief of the symptoms of ADHD when Strattera was given at a dose of 1.2 to 1.8 milligrams per kilogram of body weight per day. The drug was not effective when a smaller dose was used and there was little difference in the performance of children when using higher doses. If a forty-two pound (twenty kilogram) child were given 1.2 milligrams of Strattera per kilogram of body weight per day, he would receive a daily dose of 24 milligrams. This medication comes in 18, 25, 40, 60, and 80 milligram capsules. While the manufacturer now recommends once-a-day dosing, most of the children in the controlled studies were on a twice-a-day dosage schedule.

Use of this medication at the present time will probably be limited to situations where there is no response to stimulant medication, when parents are absolutely opposed to use of stimulant medication, when tic disorders are present, when there is a history of drug abuse in the family, or when there are significant side effects to stimulants. It also will probably be useful when anxiety and sadness disorders are present in a child with ADHD.

Strattera takes two to three weeks to achieve an effect and works on a level long-term basis. Therefore, it should not be stopped on holidays and weekends. It is not a controlled substance and a doctor can write it on a regular prescription pad.

Side effects include sleepiness and decreased appetite. The loss of appetite leads to a decrease in weight for about three months in some patients, after which weight gain reportedly resumes. Weight loss tends to be dose related. This medication does not cause insomnia. In some children Strattera causes severe stomachache and vomiting. This problem may decrease or disappear if the medication is given after a meal.

Only the test of time will determine if Strattera will become a first-line medication. The experience with Cylert and liver failure teaches us that only with an extended period of time will some unusual consequences of a given medicine make themselves known. However, Strattera certainly appears to be a clear alternative to stimulant medication.

Wellbutrin

Wellbutrin (bupropion) has gained some attention as a treatment of ADHD in several small clinical trials. In the past, I have tried this drug when all else has failed. It worked effectively in several children who had previously been resistant to other medicines.

However, there are definite drawbacks to the use of Wellbutrin. Dizziness and tremor occurred in about 7 percent of the patients. Of greater concern are seizures, which may occur in four out of every thousand persons treated with this medication. When the dose exceeds 450 milligrams a day, the estimated seizure incidence may increase as much as tenfold.

Fortunately, the usual daily dose to gain a clinical effect is around 300 milligrams a day, and under no circumstance should 450 milligrams be exceeded. If a desired clinical effect is not obtained at 400 milligrams, it would be prudent to try other strategies. Wellbutrin also comes in a sustained-release tablet that lasts for twelve hours. In this form it usually is prescribed twice a day. When prescribed in this manner, seizures occur less frequently. Tics may also occur with Wellbutrin.

Certain other drugs should not be used in conjunction with Wellbutrin, as they lower the brain's ability to defend itself against seizures. Some of these are antipsychotic medications such as Thorazine, and even some other antidepressants.

Fifteen-year-old Alicia Reed manifested many behavior problems and was being seen by a psychiatrist as well as a developmental pediatrician. Unfortunately, the two doctors never communicated with each other. The psychiatrist began Alicia on an antipsychotic to help control severe outbursts of anger, rebelliousness, and oppositional behavior. Alicia's pediatrician had run through a plethora of medications, trying to help her extremely short attention span and hyperactivity, without success. As a last resort, he gave her a prescription for Wellbutrin.

After the second day that Alicia was on these combined medications, her mother received a panicked call from the school nurse. Alicia had become disoriented, had trouble using her left hand, drooled, shook, and went into a deep sleep that lasted a couple of hours. The antipsychotic medication had made Alicia's brain more susceptible to the seizures that were a side effect of the Wellbutrin.

Wellbutrin should be avoided or used with great caution in anyone on medications that make the brain more susceptible to seizures. It should also be avoided by anyone with a seizure disorder or with a recent head injury. If a child is seeing more than one physician, there should be a close coordination of services between the involved professionals. Inappropriate care results when one hand does not know what the other hand is doing.

With the advent of Strattera the need for the use of Wellbutrin in patients with ADHD may well diminish.

OTHER MEDICATIONS
Clonidine and Tenex

Another group of medications used when the stimulant medications do not effect a change consists of Catapres (clonidine) and Tenex (guanfacine). As with many medications used today to treat ADHD, they were first produced for another purpose—in this case, the control of high blood pressure. Around the middle of the twentieth century, some medications of this type were found to be slightly effective in the treatment of some severe mental illnesses.

Clonidine was found to be very effective in treating the motor tics of Tourette's syndrome. Some of the symptoms of Tourette's syndrome are sudden jerks, blinking, guttural sounds, animal sounds, shouting out obscenities, and poor attention span. Later on, some researchers began to use this medication in the treatment of ADHD and for the control of aggressiveness, rebelliousness, and resistant behavior. In the treatment of ADHD, clonidine and Tenex affects only the hyperactive, motoric, and impulsive behavior, with little or no effect on attention span.

The most potent side effect of clonidine is extreme sleepiness. When this occurs, the dose may be reduced to a lower amount that makes a change in behavior but does not cause drowsiness. Clonidine is an antihypertensive, which means it lowers blood pressure. Blood pressure should be monitored to make sure that a child does not develop hypotension (critically low blood pressure).

The smallest dose of clonidine (0.1 milligram) is a minuscule tablet. Its small size makes it very difficult to divide into quarters or halves. We recommend that parents use a pill cutter for this purpose. Tenex, a related newer medication, causes less drowsiness than clonidine. Furthermore, it is a larger pill and therefore easier to divide.

There have been four deaths associated with the combined use of a stimulant medication and clonidine over the last several years.

When stimulant medications are used to control inattention, but do not ameliorate hyperactivity, impulsivity, anger, or defiance, some physicians add Tenex or clonidine in appropriate doses. These medications should be discontinued slowly and with caution. Too rapid withdrawal may result in rebound high blood pressure and make the child quite ill.

Aricept

On a recent visit to a state hospital, I noticed that a large number of patients with severe mental illness were smoking. Due to the health problems associated with cigarette smoking, it surprised me that the institution involved permitted this to occur. However, one of the psychiatrists said that a study many years ago indicated that smoking made people with severe mental illness calmer and less nervous. While I am strongly opposed to smoking tobacco products, there is some truth to this.

Researchers at a major northeastern university also noted this odd relationship between nicotinic acid and behavior. They began to use drugs that increase nicotinic acid for the treatment of ADHD. Several are now being used on an experimental basis. A drug called Aricept (donzepril), used to treat Alzheimer's disease, seems to help some children with ADHD, particularly in the areas of organizational and sequential skills. However, to date only small numbers of children have received these medications.

WHAT MEDICATIONS SHOULD BE USED

No one medication works on every child. Nor does it work in the same way. Many times circumstances in the child's environment will determine what medication or combination of medications will be suitable for a given child.

A February 2002 supplement to the *Journal of the American Academy of Child and Adolescent Psychiatry* states that the order of stimulant selection is arbitrary, depending on the physician's and patient's preference. However, it goes on to point out that, on average, side effect problems with appetite suppression and insomnia are greater with the amphetamine derivatives. Seventy percent of children with ADHD respond to either a methylphenidate (Ritalin) or an amphetamine (Dexedrine or Adderall) alone. If there is a failure with one type of stimulant and a trial is undertaken with another, the response rate is increased to almost 90 percent.

Kelsey Harbour was a ten-year-old fourth grader. She began taking short-acting Ritalin for ADHD, Predominantly Inattentive. Her mother gave Kelsey her medication at seven o'clock in the morning, before the school bus arrived. Kelsey ate lunch at noon and could not go to the nurse's office to take her second dose of medicine until almost one o'clock. Her teacher reported that Kelsey could not pay attention from late morning until one-thirty. Furthermore, she was very irritable at that time. Mrs. Harbour also noted irritability and agitation when her daughter arrived home from school.

At this time, the long-acting stimulant drugs such as Concerta, Ritalin LA, Metadate CD, and Adderall XR are the drugs of choice in treating most children with ADHD. There are several reasons for utilizing these newer, long-acting medications over their shorter-acting cousins. All of them eliminate having to take a pill at school. Many times the short-acting medications are not given on time, creating lapses in how well they work. For example, the benefits of Kelsey's short-acting Ritalin were effectively missing from eleven in the morning to one-thirty in the afternoon. Additionally, short-acting stimulant medications may have severe peaks and valleys between doses, during which there can be a great deal of irritability, withdrawal, or aggression. The newer, long-acting medications are distributed over a more measured and level period, eliminating many of these withdrawal side effects. With shorter-acting drugs such problems can last for an hour or two after stopping medication.

More than 200 patients in our clinic were able to convert from short-acting stimulants to the longer-acting medications with only a 6 percent failure rate.

Gene Myers was an adolescent who began to fail all of his afternoon classes. When his mother checked with the school nurse, the nurse had a full bottle of unused Adderall with the boy's name on it in her office. Going to the nurse's office made him feel different from his peers. Therefore he decided not to take his afternoon dose. Sometimes younger children and particularly young adults will fail to go to the nurse's office because they feel embarrassed.

By eliminating the second and third doses of medication, the long-acting stimulants solve this problem. Furthermore, having less medication circulating can decrease the already rare occasions when such drugs are sold illegally on the street or in schools.

Austin White began taking 54 milligrams of Concerta once a day at seven o'clock in the morning during the spring semester, and his core symptoms of ADHD improved significantly. When school began for the fall semester, his teacher complained that his attention span wavered during the last class of the day. His attempts to do homework between four and six in the afternoon became an arduous chore.

What had changed? In many parts of the country football begins in the fall and practices frequently commence at six o'clock in the morning. Band members are thrust into a similar schedule. In order for Austin to be at the football field at six, he began to take his Concerta at five. Therefore, the effects of his medication wore off by two in the afternoon.

In our clinic we recently noted that several of our male football players and band members seemed to lose the effect of their Concerta or Adderall XR by late afternoon. We hypothesized that taking the medication earlier, together with the extreme physical output of playing football or practicing in marching band, somehow metabolized the medications more quickly. Although we see this occasionally in girls as well, it is much more prevalent in our male patients.

Under these circumstances, it is necessary to add a dose of short-acting stimulant in the afternoon. Focalin may be the most efficacious as it is least likely to interfere with sleep.

Tony Jordan's mother realized that her child had ADHD. However, by placing him in an area of the house with no distractions, most of the time she could easily get him to do his homework with some minimal redirection. Furthermore, she posted important chores on a bulletin board in the kitchen, gave information in small bites, and did not become frustrated when she had to redirect her son. His father and sister supported this system and maintained consistency. Inasmuch as Tony only had occasional problems after school or on weekends, she asked his pediatrician, Dr. Cole, to prescribe Tony medication that would work only during school hours. He therefore gave Tony Ritalin LA, and also short-acting Focalin. Mrs. Jordan gave Tony the Focalin only when he had lengthy homework assignments and could not sustain sufficient alertness to finish them.

For children who need medication in the evening to finish their homework or for behavioral concerns, Concerta, which lasts twelve hours, is the medication of choice. If a parent gives Concerta at seven-thirty in the morning, there is more than enough on board to sustain the child through homework, if that task is accomplished between four and six in the afternoon. Furthermore, since most children go to bed at eight-thirty to nine, only about a one-hour gap exists before bedtime. Therefore, this is the only true once-a-day medication.

On the other hand, when children on Concerta and Adderall XR experience difficulty with sleep patterns, Ritalin LA or

Metadate CD combined with Focalin are the treatments of choice.

Occasionally a child will cause tremendous chaos in the morning before getting ready for school. With these children, every day becomes another battle to concentrate and to sequence dressing and hygiene. Families that have children with these problems are often thrown into an early morning war zone. In this situation it is efficacious to briefly get a child up and give him his medication one-half hour before his usual waking time, and then permit him to fall back to sleep. By the time he gets up his medication has kicked in and the problem is usually solved. The manufacturers of the new medication Strattera point out that since their medication works on a level basis, it is already on board, rendering the above procedure unnecessary.

CONSTRUCTING A
MEDICATION TREATMENT PLAN

A very important concept concerning medication and psychotherapy came from the 1998 NIH consensus meeting on ADHD. Groups from the University of Pittsburgh, Duke, New York State Psychiatric Institute, and two University of California campuses studied nearly 600 children. The children were divided into four groups: One group was given medication without any psychotherapy; the second group received psychotherapy only; the third, a control group, was followed in the community at large; the fourth group received both medical treatment and psychotherapy. The children were from varied socioeconomic and ethnic backgrounds. In the cluster that received medication only, parents were given guidance and support during monthly visits to reevaluate the medication.

ADHD: The Great Misdiagnosis

The children were evaluated with various tests and measurements. The group receiving medication alone and the group receiving medication and psychotherapy did appreciably better than the control group or the group receiving only psychotherapy. In children with ADHD alone, there were no appreciable differences between the group that received medical treatment only and the one receiving combined therapies. In children who had ADHD and related problems such as oppositional defiant disorder, the combination of psychotherapy and medication seemed to be just a bit more helpful.

A key to the success of the medicine-only group was the frequent monitoring and adjustment of doses in all environments. Dr. Lilly Hectman, of McGill University in Canada, noted that two-thirds of the children receiving community care actually were on medication of some kind and did rather poorly: "Commonly in the community, a prescription is written for three to six months [in my experience it is frequently for six months or longer], and there is no input from the teacher or anyone else. Compliance is not great and adjustment is not done. Medication is effective, yes, but it needs to be done systematically." This research seems to further indicate that ADHD is more a disorder of the central nervous system than one with a psychosocial or social basis. This should not dissuade individuals with associated problems such as depression (bipolar depression disorders were excluded from these studies), anxiety, anger control problems, or family issues from getting counseling and subsequent help. When mental health experts approach individuals with ADHD, they should aim therapies at specific behaviors (e.g., anger and rage) and life tasks (e.g., how to do things in a given order to accomplish various important chores and assignments).

Traditional Medical Treatments

Any medication for children or young adults should be given by a supervising adult. The dose of medication and when to take it should not be left up to the child and should be a nonnegotiable issue.

Medication should be kept under lock and key if the child is very young or depressed. While not harmful when taken in appropriate doses, any medication can be dangerous when taken in markedly large quantities. This is particularly true of the tricyclic antidepressants frequently used for ADHD. One state reported a sixfold increase in clonidine poisoning between 1998 and 1999, when clonidine began to be used for the treatment of ADHD. Overdoses of clonidine can result in extreme variations in blood pressure, depressed breathing, stoppage of breathing, and hypothermia (low body temperature).

Lastly, educators, parents, and physicians all need to observe the essential rules of the "patient's bill of rights" whenever a child is placed on medication for a behavioral disorder:

1. No child should be placed on medication or any other form of therapy without a comprehensive evaluation *in all environments.* Just last week I saw a young man whom clinicians treated with a variety of medications, high-dose vitamins, and an elimination diet. During the eight years of his treatment, no one bothered to get a good history or a psychoeducational evaluation from his school. If they had, it would have been obvious that his main problem was a learning disability in reading and written language.
2. No child should be placed on medication without a *thorough plan for follow-up* in the home, school, day-care, and

play environments. In young adults this should also include the work environment.

3. No child should be placed on medication without the
   ability to increase, decrease, or eventually discontinue
   medication when feasible.

4. No child should be put on medication without a *clear line
   of communication and plans for additional services in school,
   or without proper parent education for approaching that
   child in the home environment.*

5. No child should be put on medication without absolute
   evidence that problems with attention span, activity levels,
   executive function (organizing skills, sequencing, and self-
   monitoring), or social interaction have led to *significant
   clinical difficulty, causing clear failure in any of these areas.*

6. No child should continue on medication when *no obvious
   clinical benefit occurs.* Clinicians and parents should never
   push doses to levels that cause more harm than good.
   Rather, they should try other medications or approaches.

7. No child should be placed on medication *as a complete and
   only treatment plan.*

EIGHT

Alternative Therapies

Several alternative therapies have been suggested to treat children with ADHD. Some of these are diet therapy, megavitamin or orthomolecular therapy, biofeedback, and herbal treatments such as Saint-John's-wort and ginkgo biloba. There are many more.

DIET THERAPY

In June 1973, Benjamin Feingold, director of the allergy clinic at a Kaiser Permanente medical center in California, addressed the annual meeting of the American Medical Association and declared that hyperactive behavior was primarily associated with foods that contained salicylates and dyes. (Salicylates are chemical substances that have proved helpful for reducing pain, fever, and inflammation. Aspirin is a salicylate, as is oil of wintergreen.) Later that year, Dr. Feingold presented a paper in London that was eventually read into the U.S. Congressional Record.

Actually, his revelation was not unique, nor was the concept new that food caused changes in behavior. In the 1950s and 1960s, Speer, Deamer, and others described a disorder occurring in young adults, called Tension Fatigue Syndrome, which was related to the intake of certain food substances. The substances most cited in these earlier studies were chocolate, eggs, wheat, corn, milk, and nuts.

However, Dr. Feingold received much more publicity and attention than these earlier theorists. In his original observation, he noted subjective improvement in an adult with mental illness, who seemed to improve when salicylate ash foods and artificial flavors and colors were removed from her diet.

Based on this case, Feingold theorized that a diet devoid of both natural salicylates and food coloring would be beneficial to children with hyperactivity. In 1975 he published a popular book, *Why Your Child Is Hyperactive*. He claimed that 30 to 50 percent of the hyperactive children he treated in his clinic became free of symptoms within four weeks of the start of treatment. The diet eliminated all salicylate ash foods, a group that includes many fruits: apples, raisins, oranges, nectarines, peaches, plums, and prunes. Two vegetables, tomatoes and cucumbers, were also excluded. All foods containing synthetic colors and dyes were forbidden. This included most cereal, manufactured cookies or cakes, luncheon meats, puddings, manufactured candies, soft drinks and powdered drink mixes, tea, mustard, ketchup, many pediatric medicines, toothpaste, mouthwash, and cough drops.

Feingold believed that many hyperactive children had a genetic predisposition to abnormal reactions to these substances. He stressed that the hyperactivity disturbance in these children was caused by an inborn chemical response. In short, it was a toxic process, not an allergic response. Feingold's theory contradicts some alternative therapies for ADHD that are based on the assumption that an allergic reaction is involved in the symptoms.

Alternative Therapies

Allergy skin tests are commonly used by some alternative treatment physicians in diagnosing children who react with behavioral aberrations to various food substances.

Nine-year-old Roger Aim came to our office with his mother so that we could reevaluate his treatment plan for ADHD. Another facility had placed him on medication that no longer alleviated his symptoms. As part of his initial workup at that center, allergy testing was performed. Roger had positive reactions to corn, chocolate, beans, and milk. Mrs. Aim removed all of these products from Roger's diet, but this produced no change in his behavior. Mrs. Aim told me that she never noticed any changes in behavior previously when he had eaten these products. Inasmuch as Roger never had any noticeable reaction to this food, I asked Mrs. Aim to reintroduce one nutriment at a time over several weeks. None of these caused any increase in the boy's activity level or decreased his ability to pay attention on quantitative measures. Therefore, we tried a different medication. This change was effective and Roger is much happier and more productive.

During my medical residency, I worked in the allergy clinic at a major medical facility in San Antonio, Texas. In the 1960s, it was common for the medical residents to skin test one another under the supervision of staff doctors. I tested positive for several food substances, and the test results indicated a severe reaction to milk, yet I have never experienced any symptoms related to any of these products throughout my lifetime, nor have they in any way affected my behavior. On the other hand, we cannot rule out allergies as a factor in behavior. Children allergic to animals, airborne pollens, or other products may manifest irritability until their allergic symptoms are treated. However, they do not have ADHD.

ADHD: The Great Misdiagnosis

The Feingold or Kaiser Permanente (KP) diet became very popular, and clinicians began trials within their private practices. The therapy required strict adherence to the entire diet and its advocates believed that even a slight change from the list of forbidden foods would cause certain relapse. Because the temptation to eat prohibited items could negate success, entire families were encouraged to go on the KP plan. About the time that many clinicians expressed great doubt as to the efficacy of the KP mode of therapy, respected psychologist Keith Conners conducted a series of carefully controlled tests that indicated a slight statistically positive effect from the diet.

If what Feingold proposed was correct, it would require a new direction in how we processed, preserved, colored, and packaged food products in the United States. Therefore, in 1976 the U.S. Food and Drug Administration (FDA) authorized an interagency collaborative study on food and hyperactivity.

Several major universities were given strict testing guidelines that contained two elements. First, was there really a Feingold effect? Second, if there were an effect, was it a real phenomenon or was it the manifestation of an increased family commitment to helping the affected child?

Most of the studies indicated that there was an effect on behavior in roughly 10 to 20 percent of the children. The researchers did further testing on the favorable responders, challenging them with hidden salicylate ash foods, dyes, and placebos. Ten percent of this group also responded favorably to the diet. What this means is that out of 1,000 children with hyperactivity, ten to twenty might react favorably to the KP diet.

Later, Dr. Dora Rapp and others postulated food sensitivity as a cause of hyperactive behavior. Rapp, Feingold, and other proponents of this line of thinking have argued vigorously with each other about which food substances really cause a problem. One psychologist had videotape that showed one of his subjects going completely berserk after drinking orange juice.

Among my relatives is a man who, as a child, became extremely hyperactive and aggressive after eating chocolate or drinking cola. He spent much of his childhood eating carob and drinking clear soda. In the course of my more than thirty years in pediatric practice, I have come to respect the observations of parents. The vast majority know when a particular food substance causes their child to have increased activity levels or a decrease in attention span.

In a recent study in England, parents indicated what foods caused their children to have significant changes in behavior. The food substances were then disguised by the researcher and given to the children. Tests to determine if there were adverse changes in behavior were administered to the children and judged by the investigators. Their parents' observations proved correct every time.

Whether the cause is salicylate ash food, chocolate, nuts, eggs, milk, corn, or some other food substances, it appears that a small percentage of children with ADHD are affected by what they eat. However, the process is not entirely clear. We don't know if removing these substances from a child's diet causes only a decrease in irritability, or if an actual decrease in hyperactivity is achieved because of the elimination of a toxic reaction caused by a direct effect on the central nervous system.

MEGAVITAMINS AND
ORTHOMOLECULAR THERAPY

The current ADHD epidemic is replete with hucksters who attempt to frighten the public away from traditional therapeutic approaches while promoting their own product, most frequently a combination of high-dose vitamins and amino acid therapy. Many of these products work ADHD into their names. One patent medicine calls itself Pedi-Active A.D.D. The A.D.D. in this instance stands for Advanced Dietary Delivery. Another uses ADDition as a brand name. Those who advocate the orthomolecular approach contend that many children with learning difficulties, ADHD, and various types of mental illness suffer from biochemical imbalances and genetic differences in how the body uses materials. They argue that taking large quantities of vitamins, minerals, and amino acids can cure the problem.

The other evening as I drove home from work, I heard the following commercial on my car radio:

"Hello, Linda. How's Johnny doing in school?"

"Oh Maggie, he's doing great now that we started him on ADDition by Vitality-Man. Remember how his teacher said he had a problem and we should take him to his doctor? Well, there's no need for that now."

"Great, Linda. Guess he really needed only an attitude adjustment."

Another adult natural vitamin product called itself Kidplex and specified that it might be of help with conditions such as ADD. Various talk show hosts touted this product with vigor, and I heard one declare: "We even have lots of testimonials from satisfied parents." However, when an expert on physical fitness and vitamins was questioned on talk radio by a parent, he pointed out that these products have not been shown to help behavior and that, indeed, the manufacturers cushion their claims with intentionally ambiguous language.

More recently, I received a tape-recorded promotion of a multilevel marketing business. The promotion mentioned a series of products from a division of a large pharmaceutical house, and stated that one of the company's products lowered a child's need for Ritalin. Parents should listen to this kind of advertising with a good dose of skepticism and both ears open.

In addition to ADD, some physicians are attempting to treat a variety of conditions with orthomoleculars, although there is no evidence of benefit. These conditions include mental retardation, autism, learning disorders, schizophrenia, epilepsy, colds, cancer, wounds, poor sexual performance, the process of aging, and arthritis.

These claims are not unlike an advertisement in the classified section of the 1851 *Evansville Weekly Journal*, a newspaper that was full of advertisements for patent medicines such as California Gold, a special mixture of sarsaparilla leaves that was claimed to cure anything from tuberculosis, women's problems, and feeling low, to adverse behavior in surly young people. Several testimonials from cured people and clinicians accompanied the claims. I guess not much has changed in more than 150 years. Snake oil, sarsaparilla, high-dose vitamins, and powder from the horn of the African black rhinoceros still cure all.

I too have been involved in studies and have seen patients on orthomolecular therapy. My first contact with this kind of therapy occurred in the 1970s, when a special educator asked me to observe and give medical care to a large group of children who were being treated with orthomoleculars by a university-affiliated physician in Houston. Inasmuch as the special educator was a dear friend and her own child was included in the study, I agreed to help treat these children and provide their pediatric care. The therapy called for measurements of various vitamins, minerals, and amino acids in the children's blood and tissue, and these levels were coordinated with a treatment plan. Sadly, none of the children improved on this regimen. It simply did not work.

When one of the commercial varieties of high-dose vitamins and amino acids was widely advertised on the radio and in other media, several parents asked if they could use that product and stop their current medical treatment. I reluctantly consented. Parents had similarly approached one of my colleagues who had an interest in developmental and behavioral pediatrics. We informally kept count of the children involved and, after a couple of months, touched base with each other. None of the children we followed received a beneficial response from the product, and they eventually returned to their previous treatment plans.

Many reliable researchers, including the nutrition committees of the Canadian Pediatric Society and the AAP, have reviewed this issue. The Canadian group stated, "Megavitamin and megamineral regimens are advocated as natural therapies by various lay healers, although there is little educated evaluation of these therapies." A careful study by the University of Toronto concluded, "Data . . . do not support the suggestion that children with ADHD have positive behavioral responses, particularly those associated with ADHD." Positive responses "were more apparent during placebo as compared with vitamin therapy. A behavioral observer documented 25 percent more disruptive behavior during vitamin therapy as compared to placebo."

Most commercially available high-dose "natural vitamin products" advocated for ADHD also contain varying amounts of amino acids (the components of proteins). Promoters of these products claim that amino acids can make a difference in how the

Alternative Therapies

brain functions and thus have an effect on learning and behavior. However, the brain has a protective mechanism called the blood–brain barrier. This prevents materials outside the brain from entering into that organ in any significant amounts.

For example, an important substance that regulates inhibition or slowing of signals as they pass through the brain is a neurotransmitter called gamma-amiobutyric acid, or GABA. GABA from natural sources has great difficulty passing the barrier between the bloodstream and the brain. Researchers developed a chemically altered GABA by slightly changing its chemical composition. GABA can only be absorbed into the brain in significant amounts in this form, rather than as the naturally occurring amino acid.

Megavitamins or orthomoleculars used in the high doses required for therapy have many side effects. When vitamin A is used in high doses for prolonged periods of time it can, like other water-soluble vitamins, gradually increase in body stores and cause toxic effects, including symptoms of fatigue, an overall sick feeling, peeling of the skin, abnormal hair growth, decreased bone density, and bone pain. Another worrisome side effect simulates the symptoms of a brain tumor by causing the brain to swell, producing headache and irritability.

Toxic effects of vitamin D include weakness, loss of appetite, tiredness, and on occasion kidney stones. Some clinicians advocated high doses of vitamin B_6, or pyridoxine, in the treatment of depression, autism, and fatigue. While high-dose therapy does little or nothing for these maladies or ADHD, it can produce tingling and loss of feeling by adversely affecting the nerves leading to areas such as the arms and legs. These effects are not always reversible. Niacin, another frequent component of megavitamin therapy, can in increased doses cause severe flushing of the skin as well as toxic effects to the liver.

Dr. Robert Haslam, from the department of pediatrics and neurology at the University of Toronto, evaluated megavitamin therapy on a group of children. No benefit was noted in this study. However, over 40 percent of the children in the study had elevated liver function that did not return to normal for four weeks. The investigators concluded that megavitamins are ineffective for treating ADHD and, moreover, should not be used because of their potential to poison the liver.

BIOFEEDBACK

Computer-enhanced EEG biofeedback is another alternative therapy practiced with some frequency and given exposure in the media. In this treatment, a child is hooked up to an electroencephalograph, a machine that measures brain waves. Computers then enhance the reading of the brain's electrical activity. A biofeedback therapist evaluates the results to determine if there is a decrease in the child's beta waves (corresponding to alertness) and an increase in the theta waves component (corresponding to inattention) during various tasks. The therapist then attempts to train the child to increase beta wave activity and thus improve concentration.

Psychologist Joel Lubar first proposed this mode of therapy in the 1970s. A few children may benefit from it. One of my colleagues, a psychologist certified in biofeedback therapy, has used the technique for many years. In his opinion, only one in four children with ADHD has brain wave patterns that can be helped by this kind of treatment. Most children do better with other forms of therapy. He reserves biofeedback for clients who have not responded to medication or whose parents refuse the use of stimulants and other medications. Biofeedback therapy requires at least a three-month commitment and is expensive. For these reasons, few parents remain sufficiently compliant.

HERBAL TREATMENTS

Some parents turn to herbs in an attempt to treat the symptoms of ADHD on the premise that they are "natural" substances, not drugs, and therefore do not have side effects. Make no mistake, herbs have components that are drugs. Marijuana (cannabis), for example, is a drug. The foxglove plant contains various forms of digitalis, a drug used to treat heart disease. From the poppy plant, we derive heroin and opium. In other words, most "natural" herb products are drugs.

If herbs are drugs, how do they differ from medications manufactured by various commercial laboratories, such as Johnson and Johnson, Eli Lilly, Pfizer, and the like? By definition, herbs are primitive materials of plant origin, frequently used to treat various diseases or to improve well-being. At times they may be extracted from plants by various chemicals, and then may be called phytomedicinals or plant medicines. An example is GBE, an extract of the gingko biloba tree prepared by the Wilmar Shwabe Company of Germany. It is used for the treatment of various maladies, including memory loss in the elderly.

Herbs are usually much more diluted or weaker than the medicine provided by the pharmacist at your drugstore. The effect of a plant varies, depending on which part is used—the leaves, roots, bark, or other structures. One part of a plant may contain substances not found in another part, and some parts may contain more than one substance. Some of these substances can cause harmful effects. An example is a bark used to treat malaria. One part acts on malaria, but a second substance contains a chemical that can depress the action of the heart.

In the United States, packaged herbal treatments and supplements may vary in potency from one batch to another. They are not regulated by the FDA or the Department of Agriculture. The plants from which herbs are derived may vary considerably in the strength or properties of their active substances, depending on where they are grown, how they are stored, and how they are processed. Furthermore, appropriate dosages for the herbs most commonly used in the treatment of ADHD are still unknown.

The herbs most frequently used in children for symptoms of inattention, overactivity, and impulsivity are Saint-John's-wort, ginkgo biloba, and kava-kava.

Saint-John's-wort

Rhonda McBride, a thirty-eight-year-old vice president of operations for a major insurance company, began to have feelings of loneliness, had trouble sleeping, and always seemed in a bad mood. She frequently felt sad and confused. Her family doctor told her she was depressed and prescribed Prozac. However, she did not want to take a drug to control her emotions. On the advice of a close friend, she chose an alternative form of therapy, Saint-John's-wort. After a few weeks, her mood swings were better, she felt happier, and her relationships with her family and friends improved.

Three months later her daughter Sally, a second grader, came home with a note from her teacher. The correspondence stated that Sally was not paying attention, talked out of turn, did not finish assignments, and was failing. Rather than discussing the problem further with Sally's teacher or contacting her pediatrician, Mrs. McBride began giving her daughter Saint-John's-wort at about one-third the dose that she was taking. When a second note was sent home a few days later, Sally's mother doubled the initial dose.

Within four weeks, Sally's teacher requested a parent–teacher conference. There, Mrs. McBride learned that Sally's behavior had not improved, and she was falling farther and farther behind her peers academically. As a result of the conference, the school tested Sally for intelligence, strengths and weaknesses in various academic areas, and language ability. This evaluation indicated that Sally had learning difficulties in reading, spelling, capitalization, punctuation, and sentence construction. The child's pediatrician referred her to a developmental specialist, who diagnosed ADHD, Predominantly Inattentive. With appropriate medication and educational remediation, Sally began to show improvement.

Saint-John's-wort (*Hypericum perforatum*) is a plant grown throughout the world. The herbal treatment is derived from the dried aboveground parts of the plant collected during the flowering season. Saint-John's-wort was once thought to inhibit a brain chemical called monamine oxidase, too much of which causes depression. More recent studies show that it prevents the body from removing seratonin, a brain chemical that gives a feeling of well-being. For this reason, Saint-John's-wort functions as an antidepressant, and is useful in mild to slightly moderate cases of depression. However, it is not useful in treating ADHD. In several children that I have seen on this herb, I have noticed no signs of clinical improvement.

Side effects of Saint-John's-wort include feelings of fullness and constipation. Experiments in animals suggest unusual sensitivity to light. Therefore, it might be prudent to avoid prolonged exposure to sunlight that might lead to burning. Furthermore, Saint-John's-wort may cause several severe side effects when taken along with medications that act adversely with monamine oxidase inhibitors (MAOIs). This includes many prescription and over-the-counter medications. Anyone taking Saint-John's-wort should carefully read the labels of all over-the-counter medications to make sure they do not interact harmfully with MAOIs.

Ginkgo Biloba

Looking up ginkgo biloba on the World Wide Web, I learned that one company was marketing it as "the smart herb." Among other claims was that it increased memory in older adults with Alzheimer's disease, as well as those with hardening of the arteries of the brain. The herb contains chemicals called ginkgolides that, among other things, actually increase blood flow to the central nervous system. There have been multiple studies of ginkgo biloba in Germany using a concentrated, standardized extract of plant leaves. Although challenged by some German scientists, these studies seem to indicate that ginkgo biloba actually does help improve memory in the afflicted elderly with moderate to severe impairment. It has not resulted in benefit to those with slight or no memory loss.

However, no studies indicate that there is any improvement in memory, attention span, increased activity, or learning in children taking this drug. To reach the conclusion that ginkgo biloba can benefit children with ADHD is a giant leap of faith without scientific proof. Nonetheless, I encounter promotional information and tapes claiming that ginkgo biloba, as a part of various formulas, can help or cure children with ADHD.

Side effects of ginkgo biloba are rare. They may include headaches, stomachaches, or skin allergy. Ginkgo biloba may be dangerous to people on anticoagulant medication or with conditions that can lead to bleeding (e.g., ulcers, hemophilia), because it contains factors that might interfere with blood clots.

Kava-Kava

Richard Escobar was a four-year-old whirling dervish. He had an attention span of three to four minutes when attempting to do an activity. Furthermore, he struck out at others, including his parents and baby sister. Rarely did he fall asleep before one or two in the morning. His parents worked with a psychologist on improving their parenting skills and behavior management. However, even after several months, they had made little headway changing the child's behavior or sleeping patterns. Finally, they discussed their problem with Richard's uncle, a chiropractor. The uncle contacted a practitioner who used diet control and herbs. Richard was started on a combination of kava-kava and Saint-John's-wort. Mr. and Mrs. Escobar noted they could get their son to sleep by midnight and saw some minimal improvement in his maladaptive behaviors. This minimal improvement lasted for three weeks, after which Richard was back to his old aggressive behaviors and a two A.M. bedtime.

Kava-kava (*Piper methysticum*), a shrub, has chemicals called kava lactones that are its active ingredient. It is used primarily to treat anxiety and insomnia. Kava-kava should not be used in children or adults who are depressed, because the drug can increase the danger of suicide. Furthermore, it can increase the effects of medications used for seizures and behavior management. Problems with vision and equilibrium, a yellow staining of the skin, and rash have also been reported. More recently, the herb was implicated in several cases of liver toxicity in Germany and Switzerland. For this reason, sales of kava were suspended in Britain. Two investigative studies were being performed in the United States, but because of the problems in Europe, the FDA suspended these studies. Furthermore, thirty-eight cases of adverse events linked to kava are under review. The FDA has sent out a letter warning physicians of problems related to the herb and has asked physicians to review and report any cases of liver toxicity that may be related to kava-kava. Unfortunately, many herbs such as kava-kava do not require a prescription and are sold over the counter at drugstores combined with other herbs. Therefore, the public should be warned about the potential dangers of any herbal product that contains kava-kava as one of its ingredients.

As with other herbal products, appropriate doses for children have not been established, making the use of this drug even more dangerous for that population. Obviously, kava-kava should not be used by children with ADHD or those who have problems with depression, anxiety, or sleep pattern disorders. More effective and well-studied medications exist for such maladies in childhood.

Evening Primrose

Evening primrose is an herb that has been used in the past to treat schizophrenia, dementia, childhood hyperactivity, and ADHD. There is no scientific evidence that this herb works in any of these disorders. Some reports indicate that oil of evening primrose may trigger dormant cases of epilepsy. Primrose may also act in a harmful manner with some antipsychotic drugs, nonsteroidal anti-inflammatories (e.g., Advil and similar products), some blood pressure and heart medications (beta blockers), and anticoagulants (blood thinners).

Melatonin

Children with ADHD take melatonin when they have coexisting sleep problems or if they experience difficulty falling asleep as a side effect of various stimulant medications. It is sold over the counter at many pharmacies and health food stores.

It is called the "hormone of darkness" because it is produced by the pineal gland in humans and other species only at night. This hormone may affect all kinds of body rhythms, including those related to sleep and day–night variations. It has been shown to reset the body's internal sleep clock for travelers suffering from jet lag, for night-shift workers who must sleep in the daytime, and even in blind people.

Dr. Irna Zldanova, a researcher in the department of brain and cognitive sciences at the Massachusetts Institute of Technology (MIT), showed that melatonin could even help sleep disorders in children with debilitating neurological diseases. Dr. Richard Wurtman, director of MIT's Clinical Research Center, showed that when older adults could not sleep through the night, small doses of melatonin remedied the problem. Dr. Wurtman pointed out that he was able to get the desired effect with doses much lower than the one to three milligram tablets available commercially.

In our clinic we frequently use this naturally occurring hormone with great success when treating sleep problems in children who have ADHD.

ADHD: The Great Misdiagnosis

JUDGING ALTERNATIVE THERAPIES

Alternative therapies to medication in the treatment of ADHD are numerous. They range from extract of grape seeds to sensory integration and chiropractic procedures. Unfortunately, none of them work when placed under the scrutiny of careful studies. Only diet control and CEEG biofeedback have been shown to help an occasional child with ADHD. Certainly melatonin helps children with ADHD who suffer either primary sleep disorders or have difficulty sleeping because of their stimulant medication. Saint-John's-wort may be helpful when ADHD and mild depression coexist in a child, but is not a treatment for ADHD. Megavitamin and orthomolecular therapies not only don't provide effective treatment, but some of their components are dangerous.

For a variety of reasons, parents sometimes want to avoid standard medical treatments for ADHD. However, when dealing with these nontraditional therapies, they should remember three key principles:

1. Parents should consult competent and knowledgeable professionals to make sure that the treatments cause no harm.
2. There should be some proof other than purely anecdotal evidence that the medications, herbs, or other therapies actually work.
3. Parents of children with ADHD should avoid falling victim to the charlatans who seek to exploit their needs by charging enormous fees for products and services. Unfortunately, many people will take advantage of parents desperate for treatment for their children. Most of those alternative treatments do not work.

NINE

Treating Coexisting Disorders

The most common disorders associated with ADHD in children are learning differences, oppositional defiant disorders, and mood disturbances.

LEARNING DIFFERENCES

Learning differences occur in 60 percent of the patients we see at our child study center with ADHD. Therefore, any child with ADHD who has difficulty learning, is failing, or is performing below grade level should receive educational testing to define his problems, strengths, and weaknesses (see Chapter 12).

Many of these children may not learn to read or write via standard teaching methods and thus need special programs. The most common of these are based on the Orton-Gillingham method and alphabetaphonics. Gillingham and her colleague, Bessy Stillman, said children with specific reading disabilities could not learn by a sight word method (looking at a word and then by repetition remembering it).

ADHD: The Great Misdiagnosis

They developed a system that utilizes an approach combining sight, hearing, and touch to learn letter sounds. Much of it is based on phonics, where students learn individual letters and a variety of vowel sounds rather than word families or whole words. The program advances to sound blends, four- and five-letter words, more complex patterns, words of multiple syllables, and so on. The users of this method feel that learning to blend when pointing with a finger to each individual sound grouping helps students to unlock unfamiliar words. Constant repetition and review reinforces what the child learns.

Some reading programs that utilize variants of this method are the Stephenson program, the Herman method, the Multisensory Teaching Approach (MTA), the Saxon Reading Program, and Project Read. Many schools use these methods or similar systems when teaching children with special needs and learning differences. This is important because many of these students cannot learn easily with the standard approaches. Lindamood-Bell is another system. This method recognizes that it may be necessary to use combinations of techniques to address problems with decoding, sight word memorizing, visual imaging, and language methodology.

Make sure that any person tutoring your child has a background in teaching and tutoring children with learning differences. Experience with the various programs mentioned is a definite plus.

Other modifications that help children with learning problems are large-letter text, books on tape (available through various state and regional centers), and schoolhouse modifications for spelling and written language (see Chapter 4). Highlighting textbooks is also helpful. For example, highlight important dates with a red highlighter and important concepts with a yellow one. Don't highlight every other word or the entire system will mean nothing.

Some schools use the Irlene method as part of a remediation process in which teachers use different colored transparent overlays or the student wears tinted lenses. The developers of this system claim to improve the ability to function by filtering frequencies of light for an individual with sensitivity to glare, pattern, and color distortion, thus improving perception.

I have always been skeptical about this form of therapy, although it helped a few children I followed. Recently, I bought a yellow sunglass visor to go over my glasses to help with glare when I drive in sunlight. Much to my surprise, I found letters on certain backgrounds stood out more prominently and were a bit clearer and easier to read.

It is imperative that children with learning differences get services at school to meet their needs. Some schools will deliver this by placing a child in a class with a specially trained teacher for a given period of time each day to remediate skills. A couple of schools I work with have a special education teacher visit with the child each day in the regular classroom. The teacher also works briefly with some of the other children so that the child with special needs does not feel different.

One young woman had several children with differences in her class. She considered this a challenge and learned to teach individually to meet each child's special needs and learning style. Good teachers do this all the time. Structure and appropriate teaching techniques for children with learning disabilities and ADHD within the regular classroom are important (see Chapter 12).

MOOD DISORDERS

When mood disorders are present together with ADHD some physicians use a group of drugs called selective seratonin reuptake inhibitors (SSRIs). Early on this group included Prozac (fluoxetine), Zoloft (sertaline), and Paxil (paroxetine). In June 2003, the Federal Drug Administration warned of an increased suicide risk in depressed children on Paxil. They do not improve the condition of children with primary ADHD without depression. Obviously, they improve the condition of children whose primary depression causes symptoms similar to ADHD.

Eddie Stolz, fourteen years old, had a diagnosis of ADHD, consisting of problems with attention span, hyperactivity, and impulsivity. His physician, Dr. Morgan, treated him for many years with Ritalin and clonidine. These medications, together with appropriate modifications from his school and some counseling, controlled his symptoms reasonably well until he began junior high school. At that time his hyperactivity and impulsive symptoms subsided considerably. However, he became very withdrawn, and those around him felt he was depressed. After a new round of clinical tests confirmed that Eddie had elements of mild to moderate depression, he was placed on Zoloft. Two weeks later, Eddie was suspended from school for fighting, yelling, and speaking profanely to a teacher. He was thrown off the school bus for not obeying the rules.

Although the reason is unclear, if a child with impulsivity, opposition, defiance, anger, or aggression is treated with the older SSRIs, these poor behaviors frequently get worse. This seems to occur more frequently with Zoloft than Prozac or Paxil. Serzone (nefazodone), a newer antidepressant that works slightly differ-

Treating Coexisting Disorders

ently in the central nervous system, showed better relief of anxiety and agitation than the other SSRIs in one small study. Recently, however, the U.S. Food and Drug Administration issued a warning that liver failure occurred with this medication at a greater rate than would be expected in the population at large. Celexa (citlopram) and Effexor (venlafaxine) both work extremely well in our patients without any undue side effects. Remmeron (mirtazapine), while a good antidepressant, makes children very sleepy. Therefore, for children with ADHD, sleep problems, or depression, it is a very useful medication when given once a day at bedtime. Drawbacks include weight gain and occasional carry-over sleepiness in the morning.

Ishmael Rasheen, a fourteen-year-old, was diagnosed with ADHD and a coexisting sadness disorder. When he turned sixteen he began to have severe mood swings, together with aggression and threats to others in his environment. His doctor switched antidepressants and put him on a seizure medication called Depakote as a mood stabilizer. Soon thereafter his mood swings improved. However, after four months, the young man's doctor performed blood tests to search for abnormal liver function. These tests were very elevated and Ishmael's physician stopped the Depakote immediately. After a harrowing month without a mood stabilizer, his tests returned to normal and he was started on a new seizure medication called Trileptal (oxcarbazepin), which controlled his mood swings without causing side effects.

Various seizure medications are used as mood stabilizers. In the past the most popular were Depakote (valproic acid) and Tegretol (carbazepin). Depakote, while an excellent mood stabilizer, has potential side effects of liver failure and inflammation of the pancreas. Tegretol will decrease attention span in some children, as well as cause problems with anemia and lowering the overall blood count. This can lead to a condition in which a child may have difficulty defending herself against infection.

Recently, newer seizure medications have been used as mood stabilizers. Lactimal (lamotrigine) helps improve mood in sufferers of bipolar sadness disorders. Doses must be increased very slowly. On rare occasions Lactimal causes a life-threatening skin condition called Stevens-Johnson syndrome. Another drug, Topomax (topirmate), works well. However, in higher doses it can cause kidney stones and decrease a child's intellectual capacity. A third, Trileptal (oxycarbazepine), is excellent. I have used it in several patients who experienced significant side effects with other medications. It works extremely well and has no serious side effects.

Lithium is also used by patients with sadness disorders. It is effective in about 30 percent of children. However, lithium can cause harm to the liver, kidneys, and important chemicals in the blood.

Children with a significant sadness disorder should also receive psychotherapy and counseling. Anytime a parent feels a child is a threat to himself or may cause harm to others, the child should be evaluated for admission to a psychiatric hospital.

OPPOSITIONAL DEFIANT DISORDERS

These are probably the second most common coexisting disorders in children with ADHD. Psychiatrists see greater numbers of these children because of their severe behavioral characteristics than do pediatricians or other physicians. These children have hostile, defiant behavior characterized by frequent loss of temper,

Treating Coexisting Disorders

arguing with adults, refusing to comply with requests or rules, resentment, and anger. Frequently, their behavior is intentionally spiteful and vindictive. When accompanied by lying, stealing, fighting, harming others, destroying property, not going to school, and running away from home the behaviors constitute a conduct disorder.

In addition to medication, I find it useful to use therapy to build a conscience into a child. This must be done when the child is relatively young. It is much harder to accomplish in the teen years. Interactive groups where behaviors, situations, and solutions are modeled are also helpful. Many of these groups include the child's parents, who meet with cotherapists to discuss ways to manage behavior. Some key trigger areas explored during therapy include allowing others to be first, waiting turns, sharing, winning or losing a game, handling anger at other children, handling teasing, how to act when disagreeing with others, and learning how to accept no as an answer.

The medications Tenex and Catapres, used in ADHD for control of hyperactivity and impulsiveness, are sometimes used with these children to control adverse behavior.

In the past, antipsychotics such as Mellaril and Thorazine were also used. These have severe side effects as doses increase, including slobbering, shuffling when walking, and peculiar hand movements that resemble those seen with Parkinson's disease. If these symptoms continue they can result in severe shaking and jerky muscle movements resulting in permanent neurological damage and a condition called tardive dyskinesia.

In the last ten years a new generation of antipsychotic drugs called atypical antipsychotics has been developed. While these medications were developed to treat psychotic disorders such as schizophrenia, they are currently used to treat aggressive and op-positional behavior. The atypicals also decrease tics in many suf-ferers of motor disorders. They are called atypical because they do not usually cause the severe Parkinson's-like side effects of the earlier typical antipsychotics.

The one used most frequently in children is Respiradol (respi-radone). In the May 2002 issue of the journal *Pediatrics*, Dr. Atilla Turgay indicated that Respiradol was safe and well tolerated, and controlled disruptive behavior in eighty-four children with ADHD, disruptive disorders, and borderline intellectual function. However, as with most medications in this category, Respiradol has some side effects. It can cause significant weight increase and stimulate the pituitary gland to produce increased prolactin. This hormone can bring about enlargement of the breasts in children and even produce breast milk. Another complication is enlarge-ment of the pituitary gland to the point that it looks like a tumor. In one of my patients the size of this gland did not return to nor-mal until six months after the medication was stopped.

Zyprexa has side effects similar to Respiradol. Another drug, Seroquel, does not raise prolactin levels significantly or induce as much weight gain in most patients. The medication Geodon is the most recent atypical antipsychotic approved by the FDA. It is somewhat more effective than the other medications in this group, without the side effects of lactation and weight gain. When first released there were some concerns about changes in the heart rhythm of patients taking Geodon. However, further experience with this medication has lessened these fears.

Although rare Parkinson's-like symptoms can occasionally occur in childhood with any of these, only Respiradol has been associated with tardive dyskinesia in children. Unusual and uncontrolled muscle movements occurred almost immediately in two of my patients when beginning Respiradol and Seroquel. These ceased a short while after the medication was stopped.

All children taking medications for coexisting disorders should be monitored with appropriate laboratory tests and physical and neurological examinations at reasonably frequent intervals. To do otherwise may be courting disaster.

When approaching coexisting conditions in a child with ADHD, it is first important to determine whether the related condition is the primary cause of the problem. If it is, treating the coexisting condition may correct most of the symptoms related to maladaptive behaviors.

Learning problems, oppositional defiant disorders, and depression coexisting with ADHD require appropriate therapeutic approaches—often complicated treatment plans that involve educators, psychologists, physicians, and others.

TEN

How to Find a Clinician

In the past three years the American Academy of Pediatrics and the American Psychiatric Association have published guidelines for the identification and treatment of ADHD. While having some faults, these documents can help you understand who should evaluate and treat your child.

Mary Jordan's mother sought a physician to treat her child after her school informed her of Mary's inattention, hyperactivity, and inability to keep pace with other children when doing her lessons.

Mrs. Jordan asked several friends about who should evaluate her child. They recommended Dr. Elwort Brown. During Mary's first visit, Dr. Brown told Mrs. Jordan that there was no such thing as ADHD. Indeed, he handed her a book he wrote, entitled, *Nevermore ADHD*. He explained that all of Mary's symptoms were the result of allergies, poor diet, vitamin and mineral deficiencies, and pollutants in the environment.

His evaluation required skin testing for allergies and several tests to determine the level of minerals and other substances in her system. Once these were determined, Mary's treatment would consist of a vitamin mixture he prepared and sold, followed by allergy shots. The cost of this evaluation alone was between $2,000 and $3,000, and required a nonrefundable deposit of $1,500 before Dr. Brown began his evaluation.

A physician spent fifteen minutes with Roberto Ozuna and his family, made no attempt to get information from Roberto's school, and, based on another professional's opinion, started the child on stimulant medication. When Roberto's father asked for a more thorough workup and more time to talk to the clinician, the doctor told him, "The HMOs and my physician network make me see more and more patients to meet their goals and I don't have any more time to spend with you. Besides, they don't pay me much for this kind of examination."

Obviously, both of these extremes are wrong. Parents of a child with a combination of learning problems, poor attention span, hyperactivity, and difficulty with organizational skills should interview any physician, facility, or other professional before permitting an evaluation of their child. Selecting a multidisciplinary center, such as where I work at the Fort Worth Child Study Center, is a sound decision. We employ developmental behavioral pediatricians, psychologists, a diagnostician, and a social worker. This setup exists at major universities, medical schools, and nonprofit foundations. Unfortunately, such facilities are as common as a herd of buffalo in New York City. Even private developmental behavioral pediatricians and child psychiatrists are scarce relative to the population of children in need.

Therefore, a variety of professionals, including psychiatrists, pediatricians, and some family physicians, see the majority of children with suspected ADHD.

How to Find a Clinician

RULES TO FOLLOW

Make sure the person evaluating your child believes that ADHD is a real disorder but thinks of it as only one of the possible causes of your child's problem.

Select someone or a facility willing to get information from all of your child's environments, including school, home, play, or, if the child is older, work. An in-depth history from all these places, together with a birth, development, and interaction history and a family background, is necessary. The APA suggests a physical examination, including height, weight, and blood pressure, with each visit. In addition, a neurological and neuromaturational examination should be done. Vision and hearing should be a part of any workup.

Any professional worth her salt will spend a great deal of time telling you what the problem is, how to manage it at home, what can be done in school, and which other kinds of professionals can give your child additional services. Needless to say, this is a lengthy process. The AAP guidelines suggest two to three visits. In my own experience the entire evaluation takes at least two hours and sometimes more to complete.

Can this be accomplished in a busy family or pediatric practice? If the clinician has the background, training, and interest, she can set aside one morning a week or a specific time of the day to do such workups. In some large pediatric groups, one pediatrician will take care of all the developmental and behavioral cases for the group.

Check the credentials of the professionals seeing your child. If possible, these people should be board certified or qualified in child neurology, neurodevelopmental pediatrics, developmental behavioral pediatrics, or child psychiatry. If a professional with this kind of training is not available in your community or timelines to see these professionals are too long, ask your physician if she has had any brief fellowship training courses or regularly attends seminars and meetings on neurodevelopmental and behavioral disorders. Find out if she sees a large number of children with school, attentional, or behavioral problems.

Always ask about cost. Sometimes these examinations are not covered by insurance. Do not use anyone who wants up-front funds that are exorbitant and not applicable to the cost of your child's evaluation. Evaluations for ADHD should not run into thousands of dollars. Avoid clinicians who try to sell you vitamins or other products from their office.

Anyone you select needs to show a willingness to work and communicate with other professionals. When appropriate, the local school your child attends may do educational testing (see Chapter 11). Some physicians have a full- or part-time psychologist or diagnostician in their office to do this kind of testing. If he does not, the physician should be able to refer you to a reliable one he regularly works with.

When a final diagnosis is made, a good professional has mechanisms to follow your child's progress at regular intervals in all environments. This requires cooperation and lines of communication among professionals. Select someone willing to do this.

If you do your homework, the selection process is not difficult. It is important to obtain services from experienced professionals who can give you an accurate diagnosis, lead you to other services, and create a comprehensive treatment plan for your child.

ELEVEN

Parents and Teachers

The best possible environment for a student diagnosed with ADHD is a small, structured classroom with a low student-to-teacher ratio and few distractions. This rarely exists in the public school system. The trend continues toward inclusion classrooms, under the concept that all children can be educated equally within the same classroom environment. Private schools with specially trained educators and appropriate settings for teaching children with learning or behavioral problems usually are scarce and cost a fortune. Even nondenominational private schools no longer have small classes.

Many nondenominational private schools with a general service curriculum have no special teachers or facilities for handling children who deviate significantly from the norm, and many parents who enroll their children in these institutions find themselves without any recourse. In addition, many private parochial schools become very unthcological when they discover that a child has a learning or behavioral difference. Parents may be asked to withdraw their children at the first sign of any trouble. These schools are perfectly within their rights; the laws guaranteeing special education services for those who qualify do not govern them. Private schools are not required by law to search out and test children with disabilities. When a child attending a private school underperforms and an educational need exists, the parents may ask the public school in the area where they live for appropriate testing.

Why the rush to total inclusion? The argument is that when children with learning differences, ADHD, or other difficulties are placed in classrooms with "normal" children, they learn better because they are more motivated to perform. They are more likely to copy the behaviors of children who do not display unfavorable conduct.

On the other side of the coin is the contention that most inclusion teachers are not able to give such children the amount of time-consuming help that is often necessary for them to advance and learn. Most classes have twenty-five or more children. In an ideal world, a teaching aide would be made available to the regular classroom instructor. However, most of the time this does not occur.

A few years ago a group of educators published a book, *The Illusion of Full Inclusion*. They made the point that the idea of inclusion is nothing new. It existed before federal laws mandated special help for children with disabilities. Those laws were passed because parents complained that these children were being grossly underserved in the regular classroom and filed lawsuits against various school districts and states. In response, the federal government passed legislation to protect the rights and needs of children with various disabilities.

The best policy probably lies somewhere between inclusion and special services. Inclusion, when properly done and with the use of aides to help lower the student-to-teacher ratio, works quite well for many students. However, some students, even with these adaptations, do not function efficiently within an ordinary classroom. Therefore, it would seem prudent that any comprehensive education system be sufficiently versatile to support both kinds of classrooms to meet the pupils' needs.

In the current era, many special classrooms exist for gifted and talented students. Is this not really a form of exclusionary education meeting a special need? Frequently, these classrooms have lower student-to-teacher ratios and an accelerated curriculum that permits gifted youngsters to achieve at a more rapid pace. No less support should be available for children with learning and attentional differences. In both instances, such special classes promote success. For the child with learning differences or ADHD, they also frequently mean avoiding the agony of failure.

Ten-year-old Larry Malone attended a school that at one time operated with an open-classroom concept. In other words, several classes met simultaneously within one room. Casual barriers rather than walls separated the classes. When this system of education caused too much chaos and confusion, the school board decided to subdivide the open room into several separate spaces by using thin, temporary walls only five feet tall.

Larry had previously attended a different school with standard, self-contained classrooms, and he had few problems in that setting. However, in his new school environment, noise and instructions from adjacent areas permeated the makeshift barriers. His grades gradually began to fall. Before long, Larry's teachers asked for an evaluation to determine if he had an attentional disorder. His parents eventually found that the solution to Larry's problem was not medication, but rather getting him into a standard classroom that had fewer distractions and more structure.

The open or partially separated classroom has absolutely no place in the educational management of a child with any form of ADHD. Those sorts of classrooms should be avoided like the plague. When a school system has no regular self-contained classrooms, an alternative placement becomes imperative.

What can parents do to maximize the potential of children with ADHD? First of all, they need to remind educators that ADHD is not a simple disorder. Many important processes we take for granted are dysfunctional in these children, including attention span, activity levels, cognitive processing (learning), executive function (e.g., sequencing, organizational skills, and self-monitoring), memory, coordination, and social interaction. Second, children with true ADHD, which is based in the central nervous system, cannot help some of their problems. Through structure, appropriate modifications to the child's environment, and task-specific compensatory behavior, children with this disorder can overcome many of their obstacles.

Children with ADHD or learning differences, as well as those with various neurobehavioral disorders, have difficulty with pragmatic language, the mechanism by which children linguistically interpret instructions, reactions, others' feelings, social cues, and humor. Furthermore, it controls their own ability to have verbal interactions in social settings.

In the classroom, these children have difficulty making requests, responding to instruction, describing events, and acknowledging others. For example, when a child with these problems does not understand a question or assignment, he may state that the lesson is stupid, throw his books on the floor, or put his head on the desk. These children will do almost anything rather than

Parents and Teachers

ask for clarification. They also reason, "If I ask, I will look foolish in front of my peers."

When a teacher in an inclusion classroom knows that she has a child with ADHD or learning differences, she must explain, explain, explain until she is sure that everyone understands her instructions. She should never ask, "Weren't you listening?" Instead, without making a comment or a value judgment, she should repeat the assignment in different words.

In general, teachers should establish good, firm classroom rules when the school year begins. Making sure all the students understand the rules and know the teacher's expectations for their performance is essential. Task guidelines and procedures should be clear and known in advance. Teachers should frequently review and reinforce these parameters throughout the year. Rules should be specific and should apply to all the necessary areas.

Lynn Chen fought with another girl on the playground. Indignant when punished by her teacher, Lynn complained, "You told me it was against the rules to fight in school, but you didn't tell me anything about the playground."

Shante Monroe, a nine-year-old boy I saw in my private practice, spent the first two months of school sitting in the back of the class. He was previously identified as ADHD, Predominantly Inattentive, and in his own little world. He did not interact socially or academically with classmates. Because he made no disturbance of any kind, no one paid much attention to him until it became apparent that he was not doing class work and was failing.

Parents should make sure that their children with ADHD are positioned in a classroom area with minimal outside distractions and where a teacher can easily make sure they are paying attention. Sitting near the teacher's desk is often helpful. Avoid areas containing distractions such as pencil sharpeners, windows, doorways, or active learning centers. Occasionally, students with ADHD will need to work in study carrels (desks with three side extensions to help screen out distractions in the environment). Teachers should check the carrels at intervals to make sure the child is staying on task.

A quiet learning environment without background music and noisy machinery helps. If an air conditioner makes noise or the fluorescent lights buzz and flicker, make sure they are fixed as soon as possible.

CLASSROOM TECHNIQUES
Redirection

Appropriate interaction between the teacher and student with ADHD will often help tune the student back in. If a child seems off task or inattentive, sometimes just moving into close proximity to the child will cause some redirection.

Manual Cuing

Manual cuing, such as a soft tap on the shoulder or gesticulating, together with a direct, clear, verbal instruction, can also produce the desired effect.

Complimenting

Frequently, positive reinforcement for a specific behavior is beneficial. For example, a teacher could say, "Frank, you sure finished that history project right on time. That's really great."

Parents and Teachers

Another technique to use when a student goes off task is to compliment the other students in the immediate area who are staying on task: "Mary, I'm so glad you are paying attention to your assignment. Keep up the good work." Hearing the compliment to attentive students in the area, the inattentive student may return to task. If this does not occur, the student may be redirected by restating the suitable behavior, but without mentioning the noncompliant student's name.

Secret Codes

Some teachers develop secret cues or codes with inattentive students. When these students are off task, the teacher uses the secret code to signal them to redirect their energies or go to a safe place for a short period of time.

TOLERANCE

Many students with ADHD, Predominantly Hyperactive-Impulsive, or ADHD, Combined, tend to be very motoric—in other words, they move around a lot—but there is a difference between being motoric and being hyperactive. A motoric student may squirm in his chair, twist and twitch, move his rump all over the seat, shrug, and nod. Most children with ADHD can do little about this kind of behavior because it is neurologically driven. Teachers need to remember that the child is not running all over the class, calling out at inappropriate times, or hurting anyone.

Dr. Warren Weinberg, who was with the Department of Pediatric Neurology at the University of Texas Southwestern Medical Center at Dallas, points out that children with this problem frequently use movement within their own space as a mechanism to stay awake.

Parents and teachers should be tolerant of this type of behavior and tune it out. Never point out to the child in front of classmates that he moves too much. Never punish him for his behavior or make an example of him in front of his peers.

Some experts suggest giving the motoric child mechanical tasks at his desk to allow him to fidget in an acceptable manner while listening. They suggest activities such as doodling or prompting the child to write down key words.

ORGANIZATION AND
MANAGEMENT TECHNIQUES

Mark Ellison's desk at school was a mess. Papers were scattered everywhere. Frequently, he did not turn in his assignments. His teachers complained that when given a set of instructions in the classroom, Mark would complete only a small number of them. Most of his class work was incomplete. If he was told to do something in a given order, he never accomplished the task. Eventually, Mark was seen by a clinician, who found that the child had difficulty performing tasks given in sequence. He lacked proficiency in repeating things he heard and in arranging objects in an order he had been shown.

Remediating these problems in memory, sequencing, and organization required the cooperation of his parents and teachers. They were encouraged to give him information in small segments rather than long lists, and to divide long assignments into smaller subsets. His teacher, Mrs. Norris, provided specific written instructions on a step-by-step basis when projects were assigned. If a task required multiple instructions, she walked Mark through them one at a time, and she made sure he understood each step.

Parents and Teachers

When Mark used worksheets Mrs. Norris waited for him to complete one worksheet before giving him the next. Giving Mark several worksheets at a time would have overloaded him and accomplished nothing. Mrs. Norris learned that she had to repeat things frequently and give manual cues, such as tapping Mark on the shoulder or accompanying verbal instructions with gestures.

Mark's mother gave him a special book to write down his assignments for each class. Each subject was color coded: language arts had a blue separator, math a yellow one, history a red, and spelling a green. Mrs. Ellison set up a system with Mrs. Norris whereby the teacher gave Mark an assignment list each day for his subjects. After he finished the material at home, Mrs. Ellison would make a check mark. In this manner, Mark's teacher knew when he had completed schoolwork at home, and his mother knew if he turned it in.

For a full six weeks, eleven-year-old Eric Ross told his parents that he didn't have any homework. In addition, he frequently forgot to bring his books home. Only after his parents received failing progress slips from the school did they realize a problem existed. They spoke to Eric's teacher, who indicated that Eric had a string of zeros for incomplete homework. Obviously, he failed to bring home his daily assigned work. Eric's parents set up an advanced organizer to keep track of his assignments. Eric's teacher gave them the homework assignments by e-mail each week and his parents placed them in the organizer. The next time Eric came home and said, "I don't have any homework," his parents pulled out the organizer and showed him the tasks he had to complete before playing games.

"I forgot my books, so I can't do it anyway," he responded.

"Your teacher suggested that we keep an extra set of schoolbooks at home, so you have everything you need to get started on your homework."

"Oh, Mom!"

"You have everything you need. Do your work now."

When a child comes to class with a color-coded notebook or set of small notebooks, a teacher should make sure the material for that day is put in the appropriate section. This avoids backpack meltdown—that disorganized mass of papers, books, and other items jammed into the bottom of the backpack that results in the loss or destruction of work done in school. Color coding and the use of dividers or separate notebooks help preserve those things needed at home.

Nine-year-old Jamal Ricks' desk at school was piled full of books and paper from every course he had. When he was called on to read a lesson or a composition that he had written, he never could find it without a hassle or knocking over half the items in front of him.

Always make sure that a student's desk is organized. Color coding where various items belong is sometimes helpful. Furthermore, teachers should make sure that the student has only the materials on the desk for the particular lesson being taught. All other materials should be stowed away in color-coded and labeled notebooks or sections.

COMMUNICATION

Good communication is necessary among the parents, student, and teacher in order to maximize the educational experience for any child. In the situation of a child with ADHD, such communication is even more important. Teachers should not necessarily wait for a parent to take the first step. They need to walk the extra mile, initiating communication from the first day of school and continuing it until the last. Parents of children with ADHD should talk constantly to the teacher to check on the child's progress and to see if problems occur. Some educators will not communicate with you until a full six weeks or a semester has passed. By that time, your child may have fallen far behind academically or be on the verge of suspension.

Remember that children with ADHD have a much greater incidence of learning problems than the population at large. More than 50 or 60 percent of children with ADHD may also have learning problems.

Some classroom teachers believe that academic problems are just a manifestation of the inattentiveness and hyperactivity that many of these children exhibit. However, even when behaviors typical of ADHD are remediated by medication or behavior modification, problems with cognitive processing and learning remain in many children.

Parents and teachers should understand that any special programs or accommodations are not made to get a student out of work. Rather, they are put in place to help the child reach the achievement levels recommended for a particular grade or subject. This frequently requires great patience, perseverance, and work from all involved.

It is incumbent upon teachers not to make a diagnostic judgment by telling parents that their child has ADHD. A teacher should only say, "Mr. and Mrs. Smith, your son has a problem with paying attention, and that seems to interfere with his ability to learn. Perhaps he should be evaluated for this problem." A teacher should not say, "I have dealt with many children with ADHD, and I know your child has this sort of problem. You really ought to take him to your physician to get some medication." If appropriate, teachers should make a referral for psychoeducational testing, or for special education services if necessary.

Remember that a short attention span, increased activity, and impulsivity are common symptoms for a number of disorders or disabilities, some educational, some medical, and some psychosocial. Therefore, avoid making a specific diagnosis for a child until a full and adequate workup can be performed by a group of skilled interdisciplinary professionals.

At a recent meeting of the Learning Disabilities Association of Texas in Austin, I listened to Dr. Karen Waldron, professor of education at Trinity University. Dr. Waldron talked about behavior management in students with ADHD and made several cogent recommendations:

- Explain the rules to students before work begins.
- Use direct instruction.
- Provide a student with immediate supervised practice after a lesson, followed by independent practice and review, review, and review.
- Use facial responses or gestures for redirection.
- Avoid calling across the room.
- If a student is having a particularly bad day, have a "time-away" desk where the student can work alone before there are escalations of behaviors.
- Allow the student to earn rewards. This reinforces completed work. Rewards may include tasks such as running a classroom errand or going for a drink of water. Brief activity may support a student's need by acting as an outlet for high activity levels.

- On occasion, make a contract with the student about a small increment of behavior compliance. Take this in small steps. Avoid giant leaps that the student may not be able to accomplish and that could lead to failure and frustration.
- Graph students' achievements so they can see their progress and earn some sort of reinforcement.
- Use reinforcements such as praise, a small reward, or a token.

One teacher I knew used a token system. The children earned a play-money coin when a goal was achieved. Every so often she would run a "general store" (stocked with items purchased with her own money) from which the youngsters could buy small items with their coins.

Dr. Waldron recommends that teachers giving directions stand close to the student, saying the child's name if necessary. In elementary school, a light touch on the shoulder may also be needed to overcome distractions. Directions should be given one at a time, and written down as well as spoken. It is also helpful to have the student repeat the instructions, but this should be done quietly and not in front of the student's peers.

One of my patients, ten-year-old Anna Sanchez, did very well in the classroom, but on three successive days she brought home notes from the principal about fights and failure to comply with playground rules during recess. When Mrs. Sanchez talked with Anna's principal and teacher about the problems, she discovered that recess was very loosely supervised and contained little or no structure.

ADHD: The Great Misdiagnosis

Children with ADHD, especially when hyperactivity or impulsivity are present, frequently require extra supervision during free time such as playground time, recess, and even lunch. Mrs. Sanchez and Anna's principal and teacher determined that Anna should be monitored more closely during such times.

Parents, teachers, and other professionals in the school system must work together to provide the best opportunities and environments for children with ADHD. Teaching is an awesome responsibility. Good teachers do not need special education training to know that every child is an individual and that the method of instruction may have to be varied to reach any given student, particularly a student with different and challenging learning styles. In the teacher's hands frequently rests the child's sense of success or failure—whether the child feels able to overcome and compensate for various problems related to learning, and eventually to grow up to be a successful adult.

TWELVE

The Schoolhouse Legal Matrix

Working your way through the schoolhouse legal matrix involves knowing the rules of the game, alternating patience and assertiveness, and being your child's best advocate by insisting that appropriate educational testing and remedial services be given when needed.

Christina Berry had a wonderful first-grade teacher who could adapt to different learning styles. With some extra effort, the little girl passed with grades in the seventies.

When Christina began second grade, her teacher, Mrs. Parker, was intolerant of motoric activity and refused to alter her teaching style to fit Christina's needs. Furthermore, she would not explain lessons that Christina didn't understand, and never repeated instructions when the girl's attention wandered. Mrs. Berry was shocked when Christina had three failing grades on the first six-week report card. Her mother talked to Mrs. Parker, who insisted that the child was lazy, wouldn't listen to instructions, and made careless mistakes. Mrs. Berry asked the principal and school counselor to test the child to see if she had a learning problem.

The principal spoke to Mrs. Parker, who explained that the girl was very bright and just needed to work harder. A school counselor tested the child for ADHD utilizing a brief questionnaire. Based on this test, a physician placed Christina on Ritalin LA. While some of her wiggliness decreased and her attention span improved a bit, she still could not learn as rapidly as the other children in her class.

Six months passed and other than a small amount of tutoring, Christina was given little academic help. Frustrated, her mother asked for educational testing for special education services. Since it was May, the school's testing service said the girl could not be tested until the following September. After the first six-week reporting period of the following academic year, the school finally evaluated Christina.

A full month later, the school held a meeting to discuss Christina's educational planning. The diagnostician who did the testing took immediate charge and told the little girl's mother that the school could not offer any special help for her learning difficulties.

"My child is learning a year and a half below the other students in her class. Why can't she get help?" Mrs. Berry asked.

"Christina's I.Q. is ninety-two, which is in the normal range. Her standard scores or I.Q. equivalents for reading, reading comprehension, and math range between seventy-eight and seventy-nine. The difference between her I.Q. and her scores on the subject tests is only between thirteen and fourteen points. In order to qualify her for special education services as having a learning disability, she would have to have a sixteen-point difference," the diagnostician said.

Mrs. Berry was dumbstruck. She felt she had nowhere else to turn. She did not realize that two federal laws governing services to children with disabilities would have helped her child.

The Schoolhouse Legal Matrix

SECTION 504

The Rehabilitation Act of 1973 guarantees access and accommodations to adults and children with disabilities. This same law mandates accessibility to public places for people in wheelchairs. It is not an education law. However, if a major life function, such as learning, is jeopardized, the law requires accommodations and modifications in various facilities, including public schools.

Therefore, under section 504 of this act, some accommodations can be made to help children with ADHD. Some modifications under a 504 plan can include preferential seating in a classroom, extra time for tests, and help with organizational skills. All schools are required to appoint a 504 coordinator, such as a teacher, special educator, or counselor, who helps guide the program. This law also helps slow learners who do not have ADHD and are not otherwise qualified for special education services, and bright students who are learning disabled but who do not meet criteria for educational need.

INDIVIDUALS WITH DISABILITIES EDUCATION ACT (IDEA)

The second law, passed in the late 1970s, began as Public Law 94-142, the Education for All Handicapped Children Act. It guaranteed a free and appropriate education for all children, including those with various disabilities. When ADHD was called Minimal Cerebral Dysfunction, children with this disorder were qualified in a category called Other Health Impaired (OHI), because they were considered to have a medical disorder that interfered with learning.

ADHD: The Great Misdiagnosis

Changing the name of the disorder to Attention Deficit Disorder and then to ADHD created a great deal of confusion as to whether these children still qualified for special education services under an OHI designation, because many professionals suddenly claimed the disorder was mental and not medical. To remedy this problem, the advocacy organization CHADD and others lobbied Congress to list ADHD as a separate diagnostic category under the law for special education placement. When the law came up for recertification in 1988 the U.S. House of Representatives added ADD as a separate category to the list of qualifying disabilities. Some others included mental retardation, learning disabilities, speech and language disorders, and visual impairment. The recertification of the Individuals with Disabilities Education Act (IDEA) stalled when it reached the U.S. Senate Committee on Education. Surprisingly, there were community groups, educators, and legislators who strongly opposed the concept of ADD as a separate placement category.

As discussed in Chapter 2, the committee decided to ask professional organizations, groups that represented kids with the disorder, and various individuals two questions: What is ADD, and should it be included as a separate category under the law? The committee decided that current law already had a way to qualify these children and, therefore, a separate category was unnecessary. To clarify the matter in late 1991, the U.S. Department of Education issued a letter to all state departments of education, stating that when a learning disability existed in children with ADD, they could qualify for services under that disability. When a severe emotional disturbance was present in a child with ADD, he or she could qualify under the label "emotionally disturbed." Furthermore, if a physician considers that a child with ADHD has a neurological/medical disorder that interferes with alertness, strength, or vitality, the child should be qualified for special education services under the OHI category.

Under IDEA, a teacher or other educator who feels a child has a significant problem with learning may make a referral for testing for special education services. In states such as Texas, parents may make this request themselves. This is very important, particularly when educators fail to facilitate the process.

When Lucy Wright began to fail second grade, her mother met with her teacher. In the educator's opinion, Lucy was just immature and did not need any testing. But Lucy was falling behind the other students, so Mrs. Wright took matters into her own hands and wrote a letter to the school's principal requesting an evaluation for special education services. She signed and dated the letter and delivered it in person to the principal. In some states a written communication of this kind must be delivered only to an administrator (i.e., the principal). Teachers, diagnosticians, or counselors who receive such letters are not obligated to begin the evaluation process.

The school principal, Dr. Clayburn, informed Mrs. Wright that he too noticed Lucy's problems and that the school would begin the process to pinpoint her difficulties. He told Mrs. Wright that there was no charge for the evaluation.

Many states have a specific timeline to complete the testing and give parents the results—in Texas, sixty calendar days. Any request or consent for special education services must be written, signed, and dated, so it is clear when the timeline begins. In California, a parent may orally ask for educational testing and the school staff is obligated by law to help put that request in writing. Within fifteen days, the school must give an assessment plan to the parent. If further evaluation is needed, the process must be completed within fifty days from the time a parent signs a permission slip.

Within the next month, Mrs. Vargas, an educational diagnostician, administered intelligence and achievement tests to Lucy. She also observed how the little girl performed in the classroom, where she sat, and how she interacted with other pupils. The intelligence test compared Lucy's intellect to other children her own age and the achievement tests measured how well she could perform in specific subject areas, such as reading, math, spelling, and writing, compared with others of the same age and grade. The school counselor interviewed both Lucy and her mother. The school nurse tested Lucy's hearing and eyesight. A thorough medical and neurological workup by her physician revealed that the child had ADHD. While all the testing done at school was free, the school did not pay for the visits to the child's physician.

Three weeks after the little girl's testing was completed the school contacted Mr. and Mrs. Wright to set up a meeting to discuss the results of the evaluation and establish an individual education plan (IEP) to meet Lucy's needs.

When the Wrights entered the meeting, they met an assortment of educators, including the child's teacher, a special educator, the school counselor, the diagnostician who tested Lucy, and the principal. Results of the testing revealed Lucy had an average intelligence of ninety-eight and standard scores (I.Q. equivalents) of eighty-four in written language and reading comprehension. Mrs. Vargas, the diagnostician, acted as the chair of the committee and informed the Wrights that their daughter did not qualify for special education as learning disabled.

"However, Lucy's pediatrician faxed us a form specifying that Lucy has ADHD. He considers this to be a neurological disorder that causes decreased alertness, and therefore we can offer her special education services under what is called the 'Other Health Impaired' category." At the end of the meeting, the diagnostician gave the Wrights a copy of their daughter's testing and IEP. The IEP specified the array of special education services that Lucy would receive and how classes would be modified to meet her needs. This help would take place in a regular (inclusion) classroom to the greatest extent possible.

The committee explained that the IEP must be reviewed periodically and as necessary, at least once a year. The team or Lucy's parents could call a meeting sooner if the girl did not make progress toward her annual goals, her parents had new information that might affect her education, or she had unanticipated needs. After three years, the school would once again evaluate Lucy completely.

The IEP specified that in areas where the girl was working at grade level, she would take the state-required exit testing just as any other pupil. In specific areas where she was significantly behind her peers, a special test designed to determine if she met her annual goals would be given.

Many states do this testing periodically. A child who fails at a certain level may go to summer school and take the test again. If he fails a second time, he is not promoted to the next grade. In some states, a young adult may not be able to graduate high school if the state-required exit testing is not passed, even if the student passed all the required class work. Only an evaluating committee that makes up an IEP can overrule these requirements.

When a child is failing or working below grade level, schools are obligated to test the student to identify the problem and offer remediation. If a youngster barely passes, and her parents utilize an extraordinary amount of private tutoring, a school still may be obligated to evaluate the child as well. In cases where a school strongly feels a child does not have a disability, it may refuse to conduct an evaluation, but must give the parents a reason for its refusal in writing and inform the parents of the child's right to an independent outside evaluation.

What would happen if the school refused Lucy services, or the Wrights disagreed with the committee's findings? The evaluating committee's process is not one of majority rule, but rather of consensus. The idea is to write an IEP acceptable to both the parents and the school district. If parents disagree with a plan, they should not sign off on it. When differences in opinion cannot be resolved, a parent can ask for mediation by an outside educator. If this course of action is chosen, it is important to make sure that the school district will accept the decision of the mediator.

If all else fails, parents may ask for a due process hearing. This is a legal process involving attorneys and eventually may be settled in a court of law. Parents can sometimes obtain legal aid at little cost from attorneys who work for advocacy groups.

Unlike public institutions, private schools are not obligated to test or offer special education services. However, a child's school district is obligated to test for special education services and offer any needed services if a student transfers to a public school. Public schools are under no obligation to offer any special help in the private school setting.

Very few private schools offer much help to children with learning differences. Occasionally, more flexible ones will offer help from their own staff to aid children with ADHD or academic problems. A small number of private schools will employ special educators or find volunteers, such as retired special education teachers, to work with these children.

At age fourteen, a child receiving special education services is given a transitional plan. This plan acts as a bridge between schooling, a teenager's capabilities, and goals for adulthood. As much as possible, a young adult should participate in the process and express her educational wishes and occupational interests for the future. This transition plan paves the way for specific courses of study, such as vocational training or college preparation. Transitional planning also helps familiarize families with other services and agencies in the community.

When a young adult turns seventeen, his school must inform him of his rights relative to educational choices. When that youngster reaches eighteen, he has the right to make all further educational decisions. The only exception is if a child is sufficiently handicapped that parents establish a guardianship or power of attorney. Even though the decision-making authority is removed from the parents, they still receive all meeting notifications relevant to their child's special services.

The U.S. Congress is in the process of changing some parts of IDEA. One revision tells schools not to be entirely dependant upon a marked difference between a child's intelligence and achievement scores (in various specific subjects, such as reading and math) to decide if a child has a learning disability.

It also encourages schools to use intensive new and improved teaching methods (called research based interventions) to teach low performing students before evaluating them for special education services. Some experts reason that many of these students from either poor performance schools or deficient learning backgrounds will catch up to their peers and not require further special education testing and services.

At this time the law does not provide a deadline to accomplish this task. Therefore, some advocates fear this may be used to delay services for some students.

SPECIAL TIPS FOR COMMUNICATING WITH SCHOOLS

1. When you talk to your child's principal, be polite and dress neatly. Do not give your request letter to a secretary. Hand it to the principal in person and say, "This is a dated and signed letter [see Appendix 5] requesting an evaluation for special education services for my daughter." You might also wish to add details such as, "Her teacher, Mrs. Jones, says she is failing one subject and working below level in two others. This will also serve as my consent to do testing on my child and I will be glad to sign any forms necessary to accomplish that task."

2. Most states have a set guideline stating that your child's school must respond within a certain number of days. Parents can check with their state department of education for the number of days allotted in a given state. An evaluation must be completed within the time frame of these rules.

3. Don't be afraid to be forceful and redundant when you make your request. The squeaky wheel eventually gets oiled.

4. Keep a special notebook to record information concerning problems and contact people.

The Schoolhouse Legal Matrix

5. Maintain open lines of contact with everyone involved in your child's education.
6. Parents should never sign anything they disagree with or don't understand. Make sure to review any documents you have questions about with professionals you trust and feel have your child's best interest in mind.
7. During meetings to determine your child's eligibility or individual education plan, don't become overwhelmed, intimidated, or threatened. If you feel uncomfortable, bring a knowledgeable friend or professional to act as an advocate for the child.
8. If possible, parents should make sure their child's needs are covered under the law called IDEA. Under IDEA, schools must do a more extensive evaluation of a child's abilities to find strengths and weaknesses. Specific goals are set for the advancement of the child, resulting in an IEP that provides a wider range of programs, safeguards, monitoring, and specified times for periodic review.
9. Section 504 is not part of an education law, and as a result offers much less to children with ADHD and other disabilities. Parents should use a 504 placement only when a child has a mild problem or cannot under any circumstance qualify for special education services under IDEA.

Afterword

The front yard of my home is adorned by three beautiful large trees that form a forestlike canopy. The first, an Oklahoma redbud, came with the house. The second, a magnificent weeping willow, was from a seed, blown into place by the grace of God. I planted the third, a beautiful silver maple with three major trunks. I paid $1.98 for it when the tree was four feet tall. It cost so little because silver maples are just not supposed to grow well in the Texas heat or in our local soil. But there it is, growing every year. This year it is over twenty feet tall, with majestic green foliage and silver bark.

The maple is living testimony that things grow, develop, and thrive even when conditions are not optimal. At times when the prognosticators are all pessimistic, love, hard work, nature, and nurture can combine to produce remarkable results.

Negative statements about children with ADHD abound on the airways, in magazines, and in professional journals. Some prophets of gloom and doom say that more than one-half of the people incarcerated in American jails have the disorder. Still others claim children with ADHD have significantly higher rates of drug and alcohol abuse than their peers.

These assertions are not correct. The symptoms of increased activity, decreased alertness, and impulsivity may be the common end point of several emotional disorders. When these other conditions better explain a person's behavior, a diagnosis of primary ADHD should not be made. For example, most of the prison population suffers from conduct disorders and personality problems such as oppositional defiant disorders. These place lawbreakers in direct conflict with society's laws and rules of behavior. Many of them consciously manifest immoral, evil, and harmful behavior; they have virtually no conscience.

Children with ADHD but not oppositional defiant disorders, other personality disorders, or conduct disorders have no greater chance of breaking the law than anyone else. I have practiced general as well as behavioral and developmental pediatrics since the 1960s. I have worked with thousands of children and their parents. My patient population ranges from people on Medicaid to the upper middle class. In this extensive population, I have never noticed a greater incidence of lawbreakers, drug abusers, or alcoholics in the children with ADHD when compared to the children of my general pediatric practice.

Children with ADHD can and frequently do succeed. Parents should avoid listening to professionals and others who tell them that their child is doomed to a life of failure.

Juan Jones went to a local psychologist when he was nine years old. This psychologist frequently tested children with learning difficulties and attentional disorders. After she completed Juan's evaluation, she told his parents that they should not expect too much from Juan and that it would be difficult for him to finish high school.

Juan came from a supportive family who had a great deal of interest in education. I saw him shortly after the psychologist's prognostication. He began a course of stimulant medication, and his school provided special education services. Juan, now a young man in his early thirties, earned a master's degree in education at a major university. He is now the principal of a high school. He has not needed medication since the ninth grade.

Another young man I know, who was chastised throughout his youth for his inability to concentrate and stay still, received appropriate medical and educational intervention and currently practices law with a prestigious firm. Many of our young patients succeed in many professions and jobs requiring a variety of skills. The successes I have seen far outweigh the failures.

Some years ago, researchers followed a large group of young people with what was then called Attention Deficit Disorder, together with a matched group of peers, for several years after high school graduation. Their data revealed that ten years after graduation, there were no differences in job status or job satisfaction between the two groups. Employers did not perceive the ADD group as being any different from the control group.

As with any large population of children, young people with ADHD cover a broad spectrum of intellect and ability. They live in families who offer varying degrees of support.

Within this special population, success or failure depends on several factors:

1. Early identification followed by appropriate medical treatment, educational remediation, and other therapies. Early identification can prevent years of defeat, frustration, and failure that eventually become crippling emotionally.
2. A supportive family. Children need the encouragement of their family when the going gets rough. They need their

family to prod them along when they feel that they cannot go any further. Children should feel their family is behind them and proud of them as long as they try hard.

3. The child's self-image. Always find a child's strengths, and compliment the child on these. Many children with ADHD have a poor self-image and at times a fragile ego. Never lose faith in a child. Never tell children what they can and cannot achieve.

4. The child's individual intelligence and learning style. In any group of children, you will find a range of intelligence levels, abilities, and learning styles. These differences and how they are addressed in the classroom will affect a child's success.

5. Some young adults with ADHD can be successful at the college level. Many will need remediation, small classes, modifications, and tolerant instructors. Beginning at a community college is sometimes helpful. Several four-year universities have programs for young adults with ADHD and learning problems. A few, such as the University of the Ozarks, have a school within a school to help these youngsters. Others offer studies only for students with ADHD and learning disabilities, such as Beacon College in Florida. Still others have extensive support systems within a regular curriculum (see Appendix 3 for a list of colleges with services for students with ADHD and learning disabilities).

Children with ADHD are penalized in school for two reasons. First, their activity and attentional styles are poorly suited to sitting still. They frequently have difficulty tolerating restrictions on motion, conversation, and movement. This frenetic motor activity can irritate adults. Another problem is inattention. Children with ADHD frequently need redirection and reteaching by instructors. Some teachers dealing with large, diverse classrooms are not able to provide extra attention to those who need it.

The second reason children with ADHD are penalized in school is that many of these children have difficulty with cognitive processing and pragmatic language. Since scholastic achievement is based mostly on verbal/linguistic and mathematical/logical intelligence, children with ADHD are at a decided disadvantage in the school environment.

In 1983, researcher Howard Gardner published a book called *Frames of Mind: The Theory of Multiple Intelligences.* He theorized that there are at least seven intelligences: linguistic, spatial/visual, mathematical/logical, interpersonal, intrapersonal, bodily kinesthetic, and musical. His work should have been very important in the field of ADHD and learning disorders. However, it remained dormant for many years, collecting dust in academic libraries.

When gifted and talented programs came to the forefront in many school systems, educators suddenly realized that some children had gifts and talents that did not fit the standard categories of verbal/linguistic and mathematical/logical intelligence. Therefore, on the basis of Gardner's model, these children could be placed in specialized advanced classes solely because of their talents. The children were assessed on the basis of performance, and not necessarily on paper-and-pencil tests or a solitary test of I.Q.

According to the theory of multiple intelligences, a person with bodily kinesthetic intelligence may perform far above average in tennis, baseball, football, dance, or basketball, but not perform well in mathematical logic, which is relevant to areas like accounting, astrophysics, or astronomy. An individual gifted with interpersonal brilliance might excel as an entrepreneur or in management, politics, or diplomacy, while being somewhat klutzy. A person may be gifted in spatial/visual intelligence, and be successful in architecture or interior design, but have poor interpersonal skills. In short, this view of intelligence recognizes specialized forms of performance rather than the idea of a more generalized intellect currently held.

Many talented children with learning difficulties and ADHD can advance in various areas of nonscholastic intelligence. Very few children are advanced across all seven (or more) intelligences. Finding the talent and gearing it to future skills training is obviously very important.

Janet Lerner, a professor in the Department of Special Education at Northeastern Illinois University in Chicago, frequently tells the story of two young men. The first, Charlie, suffered terribly in school. His mother realized his anguish and decided to homeschool Charlie. While studying at home with his mother, the young man delighted in helping in the kitchen with cooking. He not only became a good cook, but could combine various different kinds of foods that had distinctive and wonderful tastes.

Recognizing the boy's unusual talents, his parents eventually sent him to a culinary school and he became a master chef. In time, he established his own restaurant. Today that eatery is considered one of the finest and most expensive restaurants in Chicago. People wait for days before they can get a reservation to enjoy Charlie Trotter's restaurant.

Dr. Lerner met the second man at a meeting for executives. This successful financier barely made passing grades in high school. However, since he was an excellent athlete and all-star football player, many universities recruited him for their athletic program. College was much harder than high school, and he almost dropped out. Only his athletic ability and all-star conference football rating kept him in school. The coaches had him tutored extensively, his courses were carefully selected, and some exceptions were made. Even with all this help, he graduated by the slimmest of margins.

After graduation from the university, he failed at his own business. But because of his charming interpersonal skills and popularity as a football player, he was afforded an opportunity to work in the commodity pits of the Chicago Board of Trade. His special abilities and talents thrived in this confusing and constantly shifting, aggressive environment.

Possessing a multifocal attention span and high activity levels, he was able to fixate on five or six transactions at once, compared to only one or two at a time for his peers. The gentleman's career soared and he made a fortune for himself and his clients. He is currently a vice president at a major brokerage house on Wall Street.

THE FUTURE

Where does the future lie for the condition we now call ADHD? For one thing, in the past few years the conceptualization of ADHD seems to be changing in the minds of many professionals.

In 1989, I met with Dr. Alfred Healy of the University of Iowa and Dr. Avrum Katcher, a prominent pediatrician in private practice and associated with the Robert Wood Johnson Medical School in New Jersey. We were lead writers for the AAP Committee on Children with Disabilities, which was in the process of writing a new definition for ADHD that took into account the various problems children with that malady possessed. We discussed the inappropriateness of the name ADHD, which was used by the American Psychiatric Association on the presumption that a limited attention span drove the syndrome. Obviously, these children had many more problems than elucidated by the nomenclature. We withdrew the idea of a name change, however, since ADHD was so widely accepted at that time.

More recently, experts such as the University of Connecticut's Paul Dworkin and Russell Barkley, director of psychology and a professor in the Department of Psychiatry and Neurology at the University of Massachusetts at Worchester, have concurred with some of our minority thoughts from that era. In a commentary in the April 1999 issue of *AAP News*, Barkley wrote, "The current consensus has largely been descriptive, concluding that ADHD mainly comprises inattentive and hyperactive-impulsive behavior. In contrast this new theory suggests that the problems with inattention are due to a biological inability to regulate inhibition. This deficit in inhibition in turn has a harmful effect on the brain's executive functions, causing poor self-guidance and self-regulation of behavioral information such as thoughts and images."

Barkley asserts that extremely young children can think only of the immediate world around them and therefore are unaware of the consequences of their actions. As children mature, they can think out their responses and behavior based on their experiences.

Executive function helps switch a person from the need for immediate action and reward to thought-out responses based on a sense of the past and what the future might hold. Executive function allows an individual to weigh long-term results over short-term consequences.

Barkley describes four executive functions:

1. Nonverbal working memory, derived from what we hear and see. Visual and auditory imagery in our memory gives us a sense of the past and future, as well as senses of time, planning, organization, and goals.
2. Verbal working memory, stemming from internalized thoughts or speech. This provides for reflection, description, instruction, and problem solving.
3. Self-regulation, which provides for internalization of emotion and motivation.
4. Reconstitution, or the ability to analyze past behaviors and then recombine what has been learned from these to form new actions.

Because ADHD delays development of inhibition, Barkley asserts, it interferes with executive functions and the "future-oriented self-regulation they provide." He concludes that ADHD is a disorder of performance rather than skill, and that the neurological and genetic nature of the disorder explains why medication is a sensible part of an overall treatment plan. Many of the techniques described throughout the book, including task-specific information, immediacy, breaking down material into smaller subsets, and using small units of information, help overcome the deficits elucidated by Barkley.

While these ideas go a long way toward explaining a full-blown case of ADHD, to some degree they neglect children who have a problem with inattention only. Perhaps these children have a completely different type of disorder that deals only with alertness. Neither does a neurogenetic theory fully explain the plight of children who have subtle insults to their central nervous system and develop the syndrome. Furthermore, the inability to gauge time, weigh consequences, and internalize experiential language is not unique to ADHD. These problems are found across a broad spectrum of other developmental and behavioral disorders.

ADHD can be envisioned as having three distinct branches. The central branch represents children with neurogenetic ADHD and children who have experienced subtle insults to their central nervous systems. The second branch consists of the imitators: medical, neurobehavioral, familial/psychosocial, sensory, and academic. The third branch represents mental disorders whose very first symptoms in an unsophisticated brain and primitive environment are hyperactivity, impulsivity, and inattention. As these children grow older and toward young adulthood, the environment becomes more complicated. They are forced to interact with their surroundings employing higher levels of thinking, feeling, language, and reality testing. Their true problems then become apparent as symptoms of disorders such as bipolar depression, pervasive developmental disorders (e.g., autism and Asperger's syndrome), schizophrenia, other psychotic disorders, schizoaffective disorder, and other personality disorders, such as borderline syndrome.

We can expect the ADHD population to grow as long as we have a drug and alcohol culture among young people of childbearing age. New technology may reduce side effects in premature infants and seriously ill children, but on the other hand, the same technology may produce more survivors with greater problems.

The ADHD population must become wary of unsubstantiated treatment plans and indiscriminate diagnoses. The lay and professional media must become more specific and tighten their interpretations of what constitutes the disorder. All concerned should understand that the symptoms of ADHD may be duplicated by many other problems and disorders.

Never lose hope in a child with ADHD. With appropriate help, these children can accomplish great things. Our ultimate goal for children with ADHD is for them to become responsible, self-supporting, independent, and self-respecting adults.

As I was writing this concluding section, my son Jonathan sent me a story written by a mother on the Internet. Her daughter, Sarah, was participating in a field day at her elementary school. Field days are rife with competitive sporting events such as foot races. The little girl's mother worried greatly that her daughter would feel defeated because she was born without a muscle in her leg and wore a brace on one foot. The mother believed that her child could not adequately compete with her peers.

At the end of the day, when Sarah's mother and father picked her up at school, the little girl smiled and exclaimed, "Mommy, Mommy, I won two races, because I had something extra."

"Perhaps the school gave her a head start," Sarah's mother thought. However, before either of her parents could comment, Sarah said, "Daddy, I didn't even get a head start. My advantage was that I had to try harder."

Trying harder, getting help early, family support, self-esteem, and acquiring alternative skills can help most children with differences to succeed.

Appendix 1: Diagnostic and Statistical Manual, Fourth Edition, Diagnostic Criteria for Attention Deficit Hyperactivity Disorder

TYPES

1. Attention Deficit Hyperactivity Disorder, Predominantly Inattentive Type: must have at least six items from the list of inattention criteria for six months or more.
2. Attention Deficit Hyperactivity Disorder, Predominantly Hyperactive-Impulsive Type: must have at least six items from the list of hyperactivity-impulsivity criteria for six or more months.
3. Attention Deficit Hyperactivity Disorder, Combined Type: must have at least six items from each list of criteria for at least six months.

CRITERIA FOR INATTENTION

The following items must be present to a degree that is maladaptive and inconsistent with an individual's developmental level.

A. Often fails to give close attention to details, makes careless mistakes in school, work, or other activities.

Appendix 1

B. Often has trouble sustaining attention in tasks or at play.
C. Often doesn't listen when spoken to directly.
D. Often doesn't follow through on instructions. Fails to finish work in school, chores, or duties in the work place (not due to oppositional behavior or failure to understand directions).
E. Often has trouble organizing tasks and activities.
F. Often avoids, dislikes, or is reluctant to engage in tasks that require sustained attention.
G. Often loses things necessary for tasks and activities.
H. Often is distracted by extraneous material.
I. Often is forgetful in daily activities.

CRITERIA FOR HYPERACTIVITY-IMPULSIVITY
Hyperactivity

A. Often fidgets with hands and feet or squirms in seat.
B. Often leaves seat when remaining seated is expected.
C. Often runs and climbs in inappropriate situations.
D. Often has trouble quietly playing or engaging in leisure.
E. Often on the go or acts as if driven.
F. Often talks excessively.

Impulsivity

G. Often blurts out answers before questions are completed.
H. Often has difficulty waiting turns.
I. Often interrupts or intrudes on others.

Diagnostic Criteria for ADHD

OTHER CRITERIA

1. Some symptoms or impairments were present before the age of seven.
2. Some impairment from the symptoms must be present in at least two or more settings (work, home, school, or play).
3. There must be clear evidence of clinically significant impairment in social, academic, or occupational settings.
4. The symptoms do not occur exclusively during the course of pervasive developmental disorders, schizophrenia, or other psychotic disorders, and are not better accounted for by other mental disorders, such as mood disorders, anxiety disorders, dissociative disorders, or personality disorders.

From the *Diagnostic and Statistical Manual for Children and Adolescents for Primary Care*, 4th edition (Elk Grove Village, IL: American Academy of Pediatrics, 1997); printed with the permission of the publisher.

Appendix 2: The American Academy of Pediatrics Definition of Attention Deficit Hyperactivity Disorder

The American Academy of Pediatrics holds that the disorders known as Attention Deficit Hyperactivity Disorders are chronic neurologic conditions resulting from persisting dysfunction within the central nervous system and are not related to gender, level of intelligence, or cultural environment. Although genetic factors or neurologic insult are sometimes indicated, the etiology in many instances is not known.

The primary symptoms in this disorder include

- difficulty with selective attention, including easy distractibility;
- difficulty with impulse control;
- problems with maintaining appropriate task-related activities;
- motoric restlessness;
- disorders of executive function, including planning and organization of cognitive tasks;
- difficulty recognizing and responding to social cues;

- difficulty attending to directions; and
- low frustration tolerance.

Commonly associated features may include, either singularly or in combination, impairment(s) in

- cognitive processing;
- sequencing;
- motor skills;
- expressive and receptive language;
- central sensory processing;
- modulation of emotional response;
- response to discipline;
- compliance with social demands;
- mood and affect.

Critical to fully understanding the Academy's position regarding this disorder is the fact that the central features found in children with ADHD occur along a continuum. Some children demonstrate symptoms of such severity that they are immediately classified as ADHD and require treatment. Other children exhibit features that do not occur with sufficient frequency or intensity to result in a diagnosis of ADHD, yet still require intervention.

Some children exhibit problems with attention, but do not have problems with impulse control or hyperactivity. These children usually have difficulty with language, learning, or cognitive processing. Because of the attention problem, they are often mislabeled as having ADHD, and their cognitive and learning problems are missed or inadequately identified.

The AAP's Definition of ADHD

Other children exhibit some of the features of ADHD along with other severe symptoms represented in a variety of psychopathologic disorders, such as pervasive developmental disorders, depression, conduct disorders, oppositional defiant disorder, and anxiety states. In these children the ADHD diagnosis may mask these other symptoms. Children may also experience specific learning disabilities that are clinically distinguishable from the ADHDs. Symptoms similar to ADHD may also occur in response to environmental factors, such as abuse or neglect, a chaotic home situation, or the loss of a significant family member. The use of therapeutic agents, such as phenobarbital or other anticonvulsants, can also produce similar symptoms. Each represents an entity clinically separate from the ADHDs.

Because the symptoms and learning problems related to the ADHDs affect children from a variety of environments in many ways, an interdisciplinary approach is needed to assess and manage the ADHDs.

The operational definition of the Attention Deficit Hyperactivity Disorder should relate to dysfunctions of attention, cognitive processing, executive function, and social interaction expressed over a period of time. The dysfunctions should be demonstrated in a variety of environments including the home and classroom. When a child experiences either a specific learning disability or intellectual deficit concurrently with the Attention Deficit Hyperactivity Disorders, the ADHDs should be diagnosed only when it can be demonstrated that the symptoms are likely not the result of the learning disability or intellectual dysfunction.

When symptoms of social interaction dysfunction are present, appropriate evaluations must occur to clearly determine if a coexisting psychopathologic condition is present.

Appendix 2

Examples of specific operational characteristics for each of the seven types of dysfunction described in the definition of ADHD follow.

1. Selective focus of attention may be shown by easy distractibility from sights and sounds ubiquitous in an educational environment, by overfocusing on activities and being unable to disengage from them, or by being unable to select the appropriate stimulus or individual that should be attended to in the educational setting. A child may demonstrate similar behaviors outside the classroom.

2. Impulsivity may be demonstrated by the inability to think of an action without performing the motor act, being easily susceptible to other children's suggestions for inappropriate behaviors, or by being unable to resist immediate action from internally stimulated desires.

3. Motoric restlessness must be documented by different mechanisms at differing ages of the child; driven, highly overactive behavior in a young child, or excessive fidgeting, squirming, or fighting behaviors in a school-aged child may serve as appropriate age-differentiating symptoms.

4. Difficulty interpreting social cues might be operationally diagnosed through the child's inability to recognize common social signals communicated from other people (lack of a social antenna), by not knowing when to stop activities in response to feelings others express, or by not recognizing signals of approval or disapproval from teachers or peers.

5. Executive function disorders may be recognized by difficulty planning, organizing, performing tasks sequentially, appropriately starting or stopping suitable activities, inhibiting activity where appropriate, or shifting from one activity to another.

6. Reduced self-monitoring awareness may be recognized by the inability to recognize what has been done, by not distinguishing success from failure in task performance or social settings, or by failing to check performance prior to initiating new tasks.

7. Low frustration tolerance may be demonstrated by the development of socially unacceptable behaviors when the child is unable to attain the desired goals or performance on expected tasks.

Other Criteria:

1. Symptoms of the disorder must be demonstrated prior to the age of seven and must be continuous from year to year.

2. Singly or in combination, a child's symptoms must be of sufficient intensity and variation from the norm of others of the same gender and ethnic background to prevent the child from achieving educationally within one standard deviation of their documented potential by age and intellectual ability.

3. If the symptoms of academic dysfunction as expressed in item two are absent, the child's symptoms, singly or in combination, must pervade the child's social/behavior interaction style to a degree that prevents the child from developing interpersonal skills within two standard deviations of expected performance.

Appendix 2

4. Although rapid advances are currently being made in electrophysiostatic and real-time imaging capabilities, as well as in computer-driven clinical diagnostic equipment, no currently available laboratory test has met any criteria to serve as a "stand-alone" diagnostic process.

Committee on Children with Disabilities, American Academy of Pediatrics, June 1991. Reprinted with the permission of *AAP News*.

Appendix 3: Colleges and Universities That Offer Programs for Young Adults with Learning Disabilities and ADHD

- American International College (MA)
- Barat College of DePaul University (IL)
- College of Mount St. Joseph (OH)
- Beacon College (FL)
- Brenau College (GA)
- Chicago State University (IL)
- Curry College (MA)
- DePaul University (IL)
- East Tennessee State University (TN)
- Farleigh Dickinson University (NJ)
- Finlandia University (MI)
- Illinois State University (IL)
- Limestone College (NC)
- Lynn University (FL)
- Marshall University (WV)
- Southern Illinois University (IL)
- Texas Tech University (TX)
- University of Arizona (AZ)
- University of Colorado at Boulder (CO)

Appendix 3

- University of Denver (CO)
- University of Illinois (IL)
- University of the Ozarks (AR)
- University of Wisconsin at Whitewater (WI)
- West Virginia Wesleyan College (WV)
- Western Carolina University (NC)

The above institutions represented themselves as having various programs or teaching aids for young adults with learning disabilities and ADHD at a postsecondary (high school) exhibit at the Annual International Meeting of the Learning Disabilities Association of America, held in Chicago in February 2003.

The services offered vary with each institution and may consist of tutoring, small classes, special modifications for learning or test taking, a special center or "university within a university," or, in at least one case, a school that specializes exclusively in young adults with learning disabilities and ADHD.

Appendix 4: Helpful Contacts and Organizations

American Academy of Pediatrics
141 Northwest Point Blvd.
Elk Grove Village, IL 60007
847-434-4000
www.aap.org

Attention Deficit Disorder Association
1788 Second St., Suite 200
Highland Park, IL 60035
847-432-ADDA (2332)
www.add.org

Attention Deficit Disorders Association SR (ADDA-SR)
12345 Jones Rd., Suite 287-7
Houston, TX 77070
www.ADDA-sr.org

Appendix 4

Children and Adults with Attention Deficit Hyperactivity Disorder
(CHADD)
8181 Professional Pl., Suite 201
Landover, MD 20785
1-800-233-4050
www.chadd.org

Learning Disabilities Association of America
4156 Library Rd.
Pittsburgh, PA 15234
412-341-1515
www.ldanatl.org

National Attention Deficit Disorders Association
(ADDA)
P.O. Box 972
Mentor, OH 44061
www.add.org

All of these organizations have pamphlets and other literature
helpful to parents and professionals. Each sponsors meetings presenting material on Attention Deficit Hyperactivity Disorder and
learning differences. The Learning Disabilities Association of
America and Children and Adults with Attention Deficit Hyperactivity Disorder have state organizations and local chapters that
sponsor support groups.

Appendix 5: Sample Letter Requesting Special Education Services

October 5, 2003

Mathew Blum, Ph.D., Principal
Mackey Elementary School
5000 Learning Road
Anywhere, U.S.A.

Dear Dr. Blum:

I am the parent of Nancy Jones, a student at your school. Her teacher, Mrs. Cable, informs me that Nancy is currently failing math and language arts [alternatively: is working below level in the following subjects]. I request that my child be evaluated for special education services.

This letter will constitute a written consent on my part to begin the evaluation. I will be happy to sign any additional consent forms necessary to begin the process.

Appendix 5

I know that in our state the evaluation is to be completed in
_____ days.

Thank you for your help in implementing this process.

Sincerely,

Monica Evans, parent

Note: If the letter is given in person, sign additional consent forms then. If mailed, utilize registered mail. If for any reason you are told the school is out of the necessary additional forms, say you will return the next day to sign them.

Notes

INTRODUCTION

p. 1 "incidence of ADHD . . ." American Psychiatric Association, *Diagnostic and Statistical Manual of Mental Disorders (DSM)* III, III-R, and IV, (Washington, D.C.: The Association, 1980–96); American Academy of Pediatrics, Committee on Children with Disabilities, "The American Academy of Pediatrics Defines ADHD," *AAP News*, June 1990, p. 12.

p. 2 "such as coastal . . ." E. Levine and B. Burke, *Social Work Today*, July 8, 2002.

p. 2 "and the Detroit . . ." Ishmial Sendi, Annual Meeting of the Michigan Youth Council, June 2001.

p. 2 "such as metropolitan Chicago . . ." Series of articles by M. Skertic in the *Chicago Sun Times*, Winter 2002.

p. 2 "the Pediatric Academic . . ." M. Rappley, quoted in Michelle Sullivan, "Stimulants Given Despite Evidence of an ADHD Diagnosis," *Pediatric News*, August 2002.

p. 3 "more than 3,000 . . ." U.S. Drug Enforcement Agency, yearly aggregate production quota, 1995.

p. 3 "doubling in the number . . ." Advertisement, Shire Richwood Laboratories, Florence, Kentucky, 1999.

Notes

p. 3 "In North Carolina . . ." 1999 Medicaid statistics, state of North Carolina, reported in Data Watch, *Pediatric News*, December 2001, p. 30.

p. 3 "use of stimulant medications . . ." M. Zito et al., "Trends in Prescribing Psychotropic Medication to Preschoolers," *JAMA* 283, no. 8 (February 23, 2000).

p. 3 "set of guidelines . . ." American Academy of Pediatrics, Committee on Quality Improvement, Subcommittee on Attention Deficit Hyperactivity Disorder, *Pediatrics* 105, no. 5 (May 2000): 1158–70.

p. 4 "that only 25 percent . . ." Deborah Johnson, *AAP News*, August 2000.

p. 4 "except Australia . . ." P. Hazel et al., "Diagnosis and Treatment of ADHD Plague Australia Too," *Medical Journal of Australia* 165 (1996): 447–80.

CHAPTER ONE

p. 7 "set strict timelines . . ." D. Kelly and G. Aylward, "Attention Deficit in School-Aged Children and Adolescents," *Pediatric Clinics of North America* 39, no. 3 (1992): 501.

p. 15 "Ed Gooze . . ." Notes, recordings, and personal conversation with Dr. Ed Gooze, Learning Disabilities Association of Texas meetings, 1996–2001.

p. 16 "deal with an argumentative . . ." A. Gooze and E. Gooze, *Operating Instructions for the Differently Wired Child* (Austin, TX: Communications and Learning Services, 1999), pp. 8–9.

p. 17 "the wiggly child . . ." Various lectures and personal conversations with Dr. Warren Weinberg, professor of pediatric neurology, University of Texas Southwestern Medical Center at Dallas, 1995–2001.

p. 19 "much greater risk of . . ." R. Barkley et al., "Driving-Related Risks and Outcomes in Adolescents and Young Adults: A Three-to-Five-Year Follow-up Survey," *Pediatrics* 92, no. 2 (August 1993): 212–18.

p. 19 "don't differ sufficiently . . ." D. Parker, USAA Insurance Co., San Antonio, Texas.

p. 20 "limits on the number . . ." National Transportation Safety Board recommendation, November 2002.

p. 22 "20 percent of girls . . ." Center for Disease Control statement, 2002.

p. 22 "teenage birthrate . . ." T. Thompson, statement, *Department of Human Health Services/Centers for Disease Control Bulletin*, November 2002.

CHAPTER TWO

p. 27 "the term Minimal Brain Injury . . ." A. Strauss et al., *Psychopathology and Education of the Brain-Injured Child*, vols. 1 and 2 (New York: Grune and Stratton, 1947–55).

p. 29 "a group of children . . ." C. Kass and H. Myklebust, "Learning Disability: An Educational Definition," *Journal of Learning Disabilities* 2 (1969): 38–40.

p. 29 "Dr. Samuel Kirk . . ." G. Senf, "Learning Disabilities," *Pediatric Clinics of North America* 20, no. 2 (1973): 611.

p. 30 "Four types of the . . ." B. Shaywitz and S. Shaywitz, "Diagnosis and Management of Attention Deficit Disorder," *Pediatric Clinics of North America* 31, no. 2 (1984): 430.

p. 31 "separate and distinct handicapping . . ." Conversations with the office of U.S. Representative Major Owens, 1988.

p. 32 "did not endorse a . . ." Conversations with administrative assistants to U.S. Senator Tom Harkin, 1989–91.

p. 32 "held meetings that explored . . ." National Association of School Administrators and the working groups and staff of the Senate Committee on Education, Washington, D.C., 1989.

p. 32 "The AAP deemed . . ." Committee on Children with Disabilities, response to U.S. Senate Inquiry on ADHD, 1991.

Notes

p. 35 "Dr. Paul Dworkin . . ." P. Dworkin, lecture before California Chapter 2 of the American Academy of Pediatrics, Palm Springs, California, March 1999.

CHAPTER THREE

p. 37 "A person does not have . . ." Various lectures by Dr. Melvin Levine.

p. 37 "in more than thirty . . ." D. Kelly and G. Aylward, "Attention Deficit in School-Aged Children and Adolescents," *Pediatric Clinics of North America* 39, no. 3 (1992): 488–89.

p. 38 "two predominant sets . . ." Kelly and Aylward, "Attention Deficit."

p. 39 "First-degree relatives . . ." Kelly and Aylward, "Attention Deficit."

p. 39 "ADHD among the twins . . ." R. Goodman and J. Stevenson, "A Twin Study of Hyperactivity: The Aetilogical Role of Genes, Family Relationships, and Perinatal Adversity," *Journal of Child Psychology and Psychiatry* 30, no. 5 (1989): 691–709.

p. 39 "exactly the same subtype . . ." F. Levy, "A Study of Twins in Australia: Genetics Plays an Important Role in ADHD Comorbidity," presentation at the annual meeting of the American Academy of Child and Adolescent Psychology; reported in *Pediatric News*, February 1998, p. 30.

p. 41 "very low birth weight . . ." J. Perlman, "Neurobehavioral Deficits in Premature Graduates of Intensive Care: Potential Medical and Neonatal Environmental Risk Factors," *Pediatrics* 108, no. 6 (December 2001).

p. 42 "subtle problems with learning . . ." M. Whitfield et al., "Extremely Premature School Children: Multiple Areas of Hidden Disability," *Archives of Diseases In Childhood* 2 (September 1997): 85–90.

p. 42 "Low birth weight is . . ." E. Mick et al., *Journal of Developmental and Behavioral Pediatrics* 23, no.1 (February 2002): 16–22.

p. 42 "many as 50 percent . . ." Perlman, "Neurobehavioral Deficits."

p. 42 "Dr. Adan Bhutta and . . ." D. Franklin, "Poor Cognitive Outcomes in School-Aged Preemies," *Pediatric News*, October 2002.

p. 43 "a study at Columbia University . . ." A. Whitaker et al., "Psychiatric Outcomes in Low-Birthweight Children at Age Six: Relation to Neonatal Ultrasound Abnormalities," *Archives of General Psychiatry* 54, no. 9 (1997): 847–56.

p. 43 "In Canada . . ." S. Saigol, "Meeting on Developmental Disabilities, Johns Hopkins University, March 1999," *Pediatric News*, June 1999, p. 12.

p. 43 "is still being analyzed . . ." Telephone interview with Dr. Saroj Saigol of McMaster University, Hamilton, Ontario, 2001.

p. 44 "Similar children in Michigan . . ." C. Hughes et al., "Cognitive Performance at School Age of Very Low Birth Weight Infants with Bronchopulmonary Dysplasia," *Journal of Developmental and Behavioral Pediatrics* 20, no. 1 (February 1999): 1–7.

p. 44 "Diseases such as leukemia . . ." R. Brown and A. Swaim, "Cognitive, Neuropsychological, and Academic Sequelae in Children with Leukemia," *Journal of Learning Disabilities* 26, no. 2 (February 1993): 74–79.

p. 44 "During their treatment . . ." J. Chessells, "Treatment of Childhood Lymphoblastic Leukemia: Present Issues and Future Prospects," *Blood Reviews* 6 (December 1992): 193–203.

p. 44 "epidemic of drug and . . ." L. Singer et al., "Childhood Medical and Behavioral Consequences of Maternal Cocaine Use," *Journal of Pediatric Psychology* 17 (August 1992): 389–406.

p. 44 "unknown to the mother's . . ." G. Glacola, "Cocaine in the Cradle: A Hidden Epidemic," *Southern Medical Journal* 83 (August 1990): 947–51.

p. 44 "one Texas county . . ." Conversations with Sister Mary Nicholas, R.N., director of Public Health Nurses, Texas Region 11.

p. 46 "Tests with animals . . ." B. Kosofsky, "Cocaine-Induced Alterations in Neurodevelopment," *Seminars in Speech and Language* 19, no. 2 (1998): 109–21.

Notes

CHAPTER FOUR

p. 47 "Many problems, disorders, and . . ." D. Kelly and G. Aylward, "Attention Deficit in School-Aged Children and Adolescents," *Pediatric Clinics of North America* 39, no. 3 (1992): 488–89.

p. 48 "other national organizations . . ." American Academy of Pediatrics, policy statement on newborn hearing screening, *Pediatrics* 103, no. 2 (February 1999): 527–30.

p. 50 "10 to 40 percent . . ." Kelly and Aylward, "Attention Deficit," 488.

p. 50 "40 to 60 percent . . ." G. August and B. Garfinkle, "Comorbidity of ADHD and Reading Disability among Clinic-Referred Children," *Journal of Abnormal Child Psychology* 18, no. 1: 29–45.

p. 51 "of 245 children . . ." P. Dworkin, meeting of California Chapter 2 of the American Academy of Pediatrics in Palm Springs, California, March 1999; reported in *Pediatric News*, May 1999, p. 37.

p. 55 "Children's Handwriting Evaluation . . ." J. Phelps et al., *Children's Handwriting Evaluation Scale: A New Diagnostic Tool* (Dallas: Dallas Scottish Rite Hospital, 1984).

p. 55 "Imagine driving a car . . ." R. Studler, professor of special education at St. Thomas Aquinas University in Houston, lectures at Learning Disabilities Association of Texas annual meetings in Austin, and personal conversations, 1996–2000.

p. 56 "Several components go into . . ." R. Duel, "Developmental Dysgraphia and Motor Skills Disorders," *Journal of Child Neurology* 1, supplement (1995): 56–58.

p. 57 "with an I.Q. below . . ." F. Castellanos, "Use of Stimulant Medication in Special Populations," lecture at the section on behavioral and developmental pediatrics, American Academy of Pediatrics annual meeting in Chicago, 1994.

p. 61 "a study of 100 . . ." W. Weinberg and R. Brumback, "The Myth of Attention Deficit Hyperactivity Disorder: Symptoms Resulting

Notes

from Multiple Causes," *Journal of Child Neurology* no. 10, supplement (1995): 431–45, and following discussion, 445–61.

p. 61 "the Vanderbilt form . . ." Vanderbilt ADHD Questionnaires, American Academy of Pediatrics Toolkit, October 2002.

p. 61 "questionnaires used most . . ." S. McCarney, *Attention Deficit Disorder Evaluation Scale, School Version*, 2d ed. (Columbia, MO: Hawthorne Education Services, 1995).

p. 67 "Seventeen percent of . . ." *Westchester Business Journal*, May 1995.

p. 71 "the loss of brain . . ." I. Trope et al., "Effects of Lead on Brain Metabolism," *Pediatrics* 107, no. 6 (2001): 1437–43.

p. 71 "Sickle-cell anemia occurs . . ." F. Oski, ed., *Principles and Practice of Pediatrics*, 2d ed. (Philadelphia: Lippincott, 1994), pp. 1515–18.

p. 72 "with iron deficiency anemia . . ." J. Halterman et al., "Iron Deficiency Anemia and Cognitive Achievement among School-Age Children and Adolescents in the United States," *Pediatrics* 107, no. 6 (June 2001).

p. 74 "*The New England Journal* . . ." P. Hauser et al., "Attention Deficit Hyperactivity Disorder in People with Generalized Resistant Thyroid Hormone," *New England Journal of Medicine* 328, no. 14 (1993): 997–1001.

p. 74 "While studies from . . ." T. Spenser et al., "ADHD and Thyroid Abnormalities: A Research Note," *Journal of Child Psychiatry* 36, no. 5 (1995).

p. 75 "For example, fragile X . . ." C. Hart, "Fifty Percent of Fragile X Patients Lack Telltale Signs," *AAP News*, 1999.

p. 78 "In 2002 . . ." R. Chervin et al., "Inattention and Symptoms of Sleep-Disordered Breathing," *Pediatrics* 109, no. 3 (March 2002).

CHAPTER FIVE

p. 83 "'One big clue to . . .'" G. Putman, "How to Get the Best from Your ADD Colleagues," *Advances for Occupational Therapy Practitioners*, February 16, 1998.

Notes

p. 84 "more than 700 . . ." American Academy of Pediatrics, Committee on Children with Disabilities and Committee on Drugs, "Medication for Children with ADHD," *Pediatrics* 98, no. 6 (1996).

p. 85 "ADHD Toolkit partly funded . . ." American Academy of Pediatrics Toolkit, October 2002.

p. 85 "'This drug didn't do so well . . .'" T. Mandelkorn, quoted in K. Battoosingh, "Scoping Available Drugs for ADHD Alternative," *Pediatric News,* March 1995.

p. 86 "almost all the new . . ." Marketing information from Celltech, McNeil, Alza, Eli Lilly, and Novartis, 2000–2003.

p. 86 "of more than 600 . . ." Advertising materials from Shire Richwood Laboratories, 1996–2001.

p. 87 "flawed and biased protocol . . ." "Algorithms of Study Come into Question," *Brown University Child and Adolescent Psychopharmacology Newsletter,* 2001.

p. 87 "U.S. Food and Drug Administration . . ." Lisa Stockbridge, regulatory review officer, U.S. Food and Drug Administration, Division of Drug Marketing, Advertising, and Communications, November 9, 2000.

p. 87 "more than 60 percent . . ." Telephone interview with Gregg Gentile, product manager, Shire Richwood, January 2000.

p. 88 "trailing only McNeil's Concerta . . ." Representatives of Shire and McNeil Laboratories, 2002.

CHAPTER SIX

p. 89 "little boy named Manny . . ." T. Armstrong, *The Myth of the ADD Child: Fifty Ways to Improve Your Child's Behavior and Attention Span without Drugs, Labels, or Coercion* (New York: Dutton, 1995), pp. 3–4.

p. 91 "smaller right frontal lobes . . ." G. Hynd et al., "ADD without Hyperactivity: A Distinct Behavioral and Neurocognitive Syndrome," *Journal of Child Neurology* 6 (1991): 37–42.

p. 91 "Children with reading disorders . . ." G. Hynd et al., "Brain Morphology in Developmental Dyslexia and ADHD," *Archives of Neurology* 47 (1990): 919–26.

p. 92 "anatomical traffic cop is smaller . . ." G. Hynd et al., "Corpus Callosum Morphology in ADHD," *Journal of Learning Disabilities* 24 (1991): 141–46.

p. 92 "area called the vermis . . ." *Brown University Adolescent and Child Psychopharmacology Newsletter*, March 2002.

p. 92 "the body's use of sugar . . ." A. Zametkin et al., "Cerebral Glucose Metabolism in Adults with Hyperactivity of Childhood Onset," *New England Journal of Medicine* 323, no. 20 (1990): 1361–66.

p. 93 "beta and theta waves . . ." J. Lubar, "Neocortical Dynamics: Implications for Understanding the Role of Neurofeedback," *Biofeedback* 22 (1997): 111–26.

p. 94 "a statement on ADHD . . ." J. Haber, B. Russman, and the Committee on Children with Disabilities, American Academy of Pediatrics, "Medication in Hyperactive Children," *Pediatrics* 80, no. 5 (November 1997): 758–60.

p. 94 "principles were reiterated . . ." American Academy of Pediatrics, Committee on Children with Disabilities and Committee on Drugs, "Medication for Children with ADHD," *Pediatrics* 98, no. 6 (1996).

CHAPTER SEVEN

p. 99 "Charles Bradley . . ." C. Bradley, "The Behavior of Children Receiving Benzedrine," *American Journal of Psychiatry* 94 (1937): 577.

p. 99 "next twenty years . . ." C. Bradley and M. Bowen, "Amphetamine Therapy of Children's Behavior Disorders," *American Journal of Orthopsychiatry* 11 (1941): 92–103.

p. 100 "in Omaha, Nebraska . . ." R. Sprague and E. Slearor, "Effects of Psychopharmacologic Agents on Learning Disorders," *Pediatric*

Clinics of North America 20, no. 3 (1973): 729; R. Maynard, "Omaha Students Given Behavior Drugs," *Washington Post*, June 29, 1970.

p. 100 "many other media outlets . . ." N. Hentoff, "The Drugged Classroom," *Evergreen Review* 14 (1970): 31; D. Dupree, "Pills for Learning," *Wall Street Journal*, January 1971; J. Rogers, "Drug Abuse—Just What the Doctor Ordered," *Psychology Today* 16 (1971): 20.

p. 101 "18 percent of . . ." R. Ulman and E. Sleator, "Responders, Nonresponders, and Placebo Responders among Children with Attention Deficit Disorder: Importance of a Blinded Placebo Evaluation," *Clinical Pediatrics* 25, no. 12 (1986): 594–99.

p. 103 "60 milligrams a day . . ." L. Greenhill et al. and the American Psychiatric Association, "Practice Parameters for the Use of Stimulant Medications in the Treatment of Children, Adolescents, and Adults," *Journal of the American Academy of Child and Adolescent Psychiatry* 41, supplement 2 (February 2002).

p. 104 "Focalin is a . . ." Y. Ding et al., "Pharmacokinetics of d and l Methylphenidate in the Human and Baboon Brain," *Psychopharmacology* 131 (1997): 71–78.

p. 104 "without many of the . . ." *Focalin Product Monograph*, 2001.

p. 105 "both types of Ritalin . . ." W. Pelham et al., "Sustained Release and Standard Methylphenidate Effects on Cognitive and Social Behavior in Children with ADD," *Pediatrics* 80, no. 4 (1987): 491–501.

p. 105 "When Concerta was . . ." J. Swanson et al., "Initiating Concerta (OROS) Methylphenidate qd in Children with Attention Deficit Hyperactivity Disorder," *Journal of Clinical Research* 3 (October 2000): 59–76.

p. 105 "called the *OROS* system . . ." N. Modi and B. Lindermuler, "Single and Multiple Dose Pharmacokinetics of an Oral Once-a-Day, Osmotic, Controlled Release OROS (Methylphenidate)

Formulation," *Journal of Clinical Pharmacology* 40 (2000): 379–88.

p. 107 "Concerta comes in . . ." *Physician's Desk Reference* (Montvale, NJ: Medical Economics Press, 2002).

p. 107 "Ritalin LA was also . . ." J. Biederman et al., data on file, Novartis Pharmaceuticals: Ritalin LA study 002, 007, 97-M-02, 97-M-03, Clinical Study and Statistical Study Report, 2002.

p. 108 "Ritalin LA comes in . . ." Ritalin LA package insert, 2002.

p. 108 "Metadate CD uses . . ." L. Greenhill et al., "A Double-Blind Placebo Study of Modified-Release Methylphenidate in Children with Attention Deficit Hyperactivity Disorder," electronic pages, *Pediatrics* 109, no. 3 (March 2002): e39.

p. 108 "used as a sprinkle . . ." K. Laban, *Journal of the Association for Child and Adolescent Psyschiatry* (April 2002).

p. 109 "altered liver function . . ." Greenhill et al. and the APA, "Practice Parameters for the Use of Stimulant Medications," 385.

p. 111 "from the National Institute . . ." *Brown University Child and Adolescent Newsletter*, September 2001.

p. 111 "Pelham and his associates . . ." W. Pelham and H. Aronoff, "A Comparison of Ritalin and Adderall: Efficacy and Time Course in Children with ADHD," *Pediatrics* 103 (December 1999): e43.

p. 112 "The FDA reviewed . . ." L. Stockbridge, FDA, letter to Shire Richwood, November 9, 2000.

p. 113 "Several hundred children . . ." J. Beiderman et al., "A Randomized Placebo-Controlled Parallel Group Study of Adderall XR in Children with Attention Deficit Hyperactivity Disorder," *Pediatrics* 110, no. 2 (2002): 258–66.

p. 114 "difference in height . . ." S. Mannuzza et al., "Hyperactive Boys Almost Grown Up; V. Replication of Psychiatric Status," *Archives of General Psychiatry* 48 (1991): 77–78.

p. 114 "In 1999 a study . . ." *Journal of the American Academy of Child and Adolescent Psychiatry* 41 (February 2002), supplement.

p. 116 "Adderall XR causes mood . . ." J. Biederman et al., "Study of Adderall XR" (2002).

p.118 "great deal of caution . . ." *Journal of the American Academy of Child and Adolescent Psychiatry* 36 (February 2002), supplement.

p. 118 "absorbed by the brain . . ." N. Volkow, medical department, Brookhaven National Laboratory; reported by M. Bykowski in *Pediatric News*, January 1999, p.32.

p. 118 "no potential for addiction . . ." Eli Lilly, Web training conference on Strattera, January 2003.

p. 119 "low levels of . . ." J. Cooper, National Institute of Health ADHD conference in Washington, D.C., 1998.

p. 119 "survey of high school . . ." "Survey Finds Few Incidents of Diversion of ADHD Drugs," *Brown University Child and Adolescent Psychopharmacology Newsletter*, November 2001, p. 3.

p. 119 "In January 2003 . . ." R. Barkley et al., "Driving-Related Risks and Outcomes in Adolescents and Young Adults: A Three-to-Five-Year Follow-up Survey," *Pediatrics* 92, no. 2 (August 1993): 212–18.

p. 120 "previously underlying and . . ." M. Donohue, "Low Risk of Death with Tricyclics," *Pediatric News*, April 1999, p. 37; D. Atkins, lecture at annual session of the American Heart Association, 1999; reported in *Pediatric News*, April 1999, p. 31.

p. 121 "a 1996 policy statement on . . ." American Academy of Pediatrics, Committee on Children with Disabilities, policy statement on ADHD and medication, 1996.

p. 122 "trials on Strattera . . ." D. Michaelson et al., "Atomoxetine in the Treatment of Children and Adolescents with Attention-Deficit/Hyperactivity Disorder: A Randomized, Placebo-Controlled, Dose-Response Study," *Pediatrics* 108, no. 5 (2001): e83; "Studies Reveal Atomoxetine Effective Treatment for ADHD," *Brown University Child and Adolescent Psychopharmacology Newsletter*, January 2002.

p. 123 "Side effects include . . ." Eli Lilly, Web training conference on Strattera, January 2003.

p. 123 "has gained some attention . . ." L. Barrikman et al., "Bupropion versus Methylphenidate in the Treatment of ADHD," *Journal of the American Academy of Child and Adolescent Psychiatry* 34 (1995): 649–57.

p. 126 "some researchers began to use . . ." R. Hunt et al., "Clonidine Benefits Children with ADD and Hyperactivity," *Journal of the American Academy of Child and Adolescent Psychiatry* 24 (1985): 617–29.

p. 127 "nicotinic acid for the . . ." Telephone conversation with Dr. Timothy Willins, 2002.

p. 127 "order of stimulant selection . . ." *Journal of the American Academy of Child and Adolescent Psychiatry* 36 (February 2002), supplement.

p. 128 "6 percent failure rate . . ." This claim is based on my experience with more than 250 patients at the Fort Worth Child Study Center, 2001–2002.

p. 131 "NIH consensus meeting . . ." MTA Cooperative Group, "A Fourteen-Month Randomized Clinical Trial of Treatment Strategies for ADHD," *Archives of General Psychiatry* 56, no. 12 (1999): 1073–86.

p.133 "One state reported . . . " G. Rogers, lecture. Annual meeting of the American Academy of Pediatrics. San Francisco, October 1998.

CHAPTER EIGHT

p. 135 "In the 1950s and . . ." F. Speer, "The Allergic Tension Fatigue Syndrome," *Pediatric Clinics of North America* 1 (1954): 1029.

p. 136 "published a popular book . . ." B. Feingold, *Why Your Child Is Hyperactive* (New York: Random House, 1975).

Notes

p. 138 "interagency collaborative study on . . ." G. Landman, "Alternative Therapies," *Developmental-Behavioral Pediatrics*, 2d ed., ed. M. Levine, W. Carey, and A. Crocker (Philadelphia: Saunders, 1992), p. 754.

p. 138 "Several major universities . . ." J. Harley, "Synthetic Food Colors and Hyperactivity in Children: A Double-Blind Challenge Experiment," *Pediatrics* 62 (1978): 975.

p. 138 "Dr. Dora Rapp and . . ." D. Rapp, *Is This Your Child? Discovering and Treating Unrecognized Allergies in Children and Adults* (New York: Quill/W. Morrow, 1991).

p. 138 "have argued vigorously . . ."Round table at the American Academy of Pediatrics annual meeting, circa 1979.

p. 139 "psychologist had videotape . . ." D. O'Banion, at various meetings of the Association for Children with Learning Disabilities (ALCD) in the 1970s.

p. 139 "recent study in England . . ." C. Carter et al., "Effects of a Few-Food Diet in Attention Deficit Disorder," *Archives of Diseases of Children* 69 (1993): 564–68.

p. 140 "an expert on physical fitness . . ." Larry North Show, KRLD in Dallas–Fort Worth, 1997.

p. 142 "The Canadian group stated . . ." Nutrition Committee, Société Canadienne de pédiatrie, "Megavitamin and Mineral Therapy in Childhood," *Canadian Medical Association Journal,* 143 (1990): 1009–13.

p. 142 "the University of Toronto . . ." R. Haslam, "Is There a Role for Megavitamin Therapy in the Treatment of ADHD?" *Advances in Neurology* 58 (1992): 303–10.

p. 144 "elevated liver function . . ." Haslam, "Is There a Role?"

p. 144 "biofeedback therapist evaluates . . ." J. Lubar, "Neocortical Dynamic Implications for Understanding the Role of Neurofeedback and Related Techniques for Enhancement of Attention," *Biofeedback* 22 (1997): 11–26.

p. 144 "then attempts to train . . ." J. Lubar et al., "Evaluation of EEG Neurofeedback Training for ADHD," *Biofeedback and Self-Regulation* 20 (1995): 83–99.

p. 144 "One of my colleagues . . ." Dr. Daniel Lowrance, 1980–2003.

p. 145 "herbs are primitive materials . . ." V. Tyler, *Herbs of Choice: The Therapeutic Use of Phytomedicinals* (New York: Pharmaceutical Products Press, 1994), pp. 108–11.

p. 145 "may be called phytomedicinals . . ." V. Tyler, *The Honest Herbal: A Sensible Guide to the Use of Herbs and Related Remedies* (New York: Pharmaceutical Products Press, 1993), pp. 149–51.

p. 146 "Saint-John's-wort functions as an anti-depressant . . ." L. Klaus et al., "St.-John's-Wort for Depression: An Overview and Meta-analysis of Randomized Clinical Trials," *British Medical Journal* 313 (1996): 255–57.

p. 147 "a plant grown throughout . . ." *Physician's Desk Reference for Herbal Medicines* (Montvale, NJ: Medical Economics Press, 1999), pp. 906–907.

p. 148 "'the smart herb . . .'" Greenfields Nutrition Ltd. website, 2000.

p. 148 "with Alzheimer's . . ." A. Wong et al., "Herbal Remedies in Psychiatric Practice," *Archives of General Psychiatry* 55 (1998): 1035.

p. 148 "in Germany using . . ." U. Stein, "Ginkgo Biloba Extracts" (letter), *The Lancet* 355, no. 8687 (1990): 45–46.

p. 150 "staining of the skin, and rash . . ." P. Ruze, "Kava-Induced Dermopathy: A Niacin Deficiency?" *The Lancet* 355, no. 8703 (1990): 1442–45.

p. 150 "cases of liver toxicity . . ." "Troubling News on Kava" *Brown University Child and Adolescent Psychopharmacology Update*, March 2002.

p. 150 "Evening primrose is an herb . . ." Wong et al., "Herbal Remedies."

p. 151 "Dr. Irna Zldanova . . ." D. Halpern, "Scientists Pinpoint Dosage of Melatonin for Insomnia," MIT Tech Talk, Massachusetts Institute of Technology, October 2001.

Notes

CHAPTER NINE

p. 153 "60 percent of the . . ." G. August and B. Garfinkle, "Comorbidity of ADHD and Reading Disability among Clinic-Referred Children," *Journal of Abnormal Child Psychology* 18, no. 1 (February 1990): 29–48.

p. 153 "and her colleague, Bessy . . ." Remediation Plus website, www.remediationplus.com, 2003.

p. 154 "are the Stephenson program . . ." Dyslexia Awareness and Resource Center, 2003.

p. 154 "Lindamood-Bell is another . . ." P. Lindamood et al., "Sensory-Cognitive Factors in the Controversy over Reading Instruction," *Journal of Developmental and Learning Disorders* 1, no. 1 (1997); interviews with Lindamood-Bell personnel at the Annual International Meeting of the Learning Disabilities Association of America, February 2003.

p. 155 "colored transparent overlays . . ." H. Irlene, *Reading by the Colors* (New York: Avenbury Press, 1991).

p. 156 "Paxil is also helpful . . ." *PDR* (Montvale, NJ: Medical Economics Press, 2003).

p. 157 "Recently, however, the U.S. . . ." *Brown University Child and Adolescent Psychopharmacology Newsletter*, February 2002.

p. 157 "of the pancreas . . ." *PDR*, 2003.

p. 158 "Recently, newer seizure medications . . ." K. Richards, pediatric neurologist, presentation at the Annual Meeting of the Texas Pediatric Society in Fort Worth, October 2002.

p. 159 "Interactive groups where . . ." T. Foster, leader of ODD Interactive Group, Fort Worth Child Study Center, August 2002.

p. 160 "that Respiradol was safe . . ." T. Atilla et al., "Long-Term Safety and Efficacy of Respiradone for the Treatment of Disruptive Behavior Disorders in Children with Subaverage I.Q.'s," *Pediatrics* 110, no. 3 (September 2002).

CHAPTER TEN

p. 163 "the American Academy of Pediatrics . . ." American Academy of Pediatrics, Committee on Quality Improvement, Subcommittee on ADHD, "Clinical Practice Guidelines: Diagnosis and Evaluation of the Child with Attention Deficit Hyperactivity Disorder," *Pediatrics* 105, no. 5 (May 2000).

p. 163 "the American Psychiatric Association . . ." L. Greenhill et al. and the American Psychiatric Association, "Practice Parameters for the Use of Stimulant Medications in the Treatment of Children, Adolescents, and Adults," *Journal of the American Academy of Child and Adolescent Psychiatry* 41, supplement 2 (February 2002).

p. 165 "ADHD is a real disorder . . ." American Academy of Pediatrics, Committee on Quality Improvement, Subcommittee on ADHD, "Clinical Practice Guideline: Treatment of the School-Aged Child with Attention Deficit/Hyperactivity Disorder," *Pediatrics* 108, no. 4 (2001): 1033–44.

CHAPTER ELEVEN

p. 167 "small, structured classroom . . ." Telephone interviews with C. Cootz, Special Education Department, Texas Christian University, and L. Hetton, former director of Hill School, Fort Worth, Texas, 2000.

p. 168 "for appropriate testing . . ." J. Haber and the Texas Pediatric Society Committee on Children with Disabilities, *How Do I Get Help for My Child with a School Problem?* rev. ed. (Austin: Texas Pediatric Society, 2002).

p. 168 "published a book . . ." J. Kauffman and D. Hallahan, *The Illusion of Full Inclusion: A Comprehensive Critique of a Current Special Education Bandwagon* (Austin, TX: Pro-Ed,1995).

p. 169 "for gifted and talented . . ." N. Robinson, "Educational Options for Gifted Children," *Pediatric Annals* 14, no. 10 (1985): 753.

Notes

p. 170 "dysfunctional in these children . . ." Lecture at the Committee on Disabilities meeting, American Academy of Pediatrics, 1990.

p. 170 "difficulty with pragmatic language . . ." L. Ellis, Texas Woman's University, presentation at the Third Annual Meeting for At-Risk Children and Adolescents in Denton, TX, 1998.

p. 171 "or a value judgment . . ." M. Levine, "Attention Variation and Dysfunction," in *Developmental-Behavioral Pediatrics*, 2d ed., ed. M. Levine, W. Carey, and A. Crocker (Philadelphia: Saunders, 1992), p. 475.

p. 171 "firm classroom rules . . ." K. Waldron, Trinity University, presentation at the Learning Disabilities Association of Texas annual meeting in Austin, 1997.

p. 171 "'anything about the playground . . .'" Ellis, presentation.

p. 171 "positioned in a classroom . . ." D. Kelly and G. Aylward, "Attention Deficit in School-Aged Children and Adolescents," *Pediatric Clinics of North America* 39, no. 3 (1992).

p. 173 "compliment the other students . . ." Waldron, presentation.

p. 173 "secret cues or codes . . ." Levine, "Attention Variation and Dysfunction," 1992.

p. 173 "frequently use movement . . ." W. Weinberg, lectures, seminars, and personal conversations, 1995–2002.

p. 174 "such as doodling . . ." Levine, "Attention Variation and Dysfunction," 1992.

p. 174 "walked Mark through . . ." M. Baren, "Managing ADHD," *Contemporary Pediatrics* 11, no. 12 (December 1994): 29–48.

p. 175 "extra set of schoolbooks . . ." Panel on ADHD and learning differences, Learning Disabilities Association of Texas annual meeting in Austin, 1998.

p. 177 "50 or 60 percent . . ." G. Hynd et al., "ADD without Hyperactivity: A Distinct Behavioral and Neurocognitive Syndrome," *Journal of Child Neurology* 6 (1991): 37–42.

p. 177 "any special programs . . ." Baren, "Managing ADHD."

p. 178 "behavior management in students . . ." Waldron, presentation.

Notes

CHAPTER TWELVE

p. 183 "access and accommodations . . ." Section 504 of the Rehabilitation Act of 1973.

p. 183 "The second law, passed . . ." Public Law 94-142, Education for All Handicapped Children Act, 1975.

p. 184 "and then to ADHD . . ." American Psychiatric Association, *Diagnostic and Statistical Manual of Mental Disorders*, 4th ed. (*DSM-IV*) (Washington, D.C.: The Association, 1996).

p. 184 "who strongly opposed . . ." J. Haber, testimony before the U.S. Senate Working Committee on Education, Washington, D.C., Fall 1998.

p. 184 "committee decided to ask . . ." Conversations with Sen. Harkin, chair of the Senate Committee on Education; Mr. Silverstein of Sen. Harkin's office; and other aides.

p. 187 "and IEP . . ." American Academy of Pediatrics, Committee on Children with Disabilities, "The Pediatrician's Role in Development and Implementation of an IEP and IFSP," *Pediatrics* 104, no. 1 (July 1999).

p. 189 "transitional plan . . ." J. Haber and the Texas Pediatric Society Committee on Children with Disabilities, *How Do I Get Help for My Child with a School Problem?* rev. ed. (Austin: Texas Pediatric Society, 2002).

p. 190 "Special Tips for Communicating . . ." C. Norris, addition to *How Do I Get Help for My Child with a School Problem?* Fort Worth Child Study Center version (Austin: Texas Pediatric Society, 2003).

AFTERWORD

p. 194 "assertions are not correct . . ." J. Biederman et al., "Pharmacotherapy of Attention Deficit Hyperactivity Disorder Reduces Risk for Substance Use Disorder," *Pediatrics* 104, no. 2 (1999): e20.

Notes

p. 195 "ten years after graduation . . ." G. Weiss and L. Hechtman, "Hyperactives as Young Adults: A Controlled Prospective Ten-Year Follow-up Study of Seventy-five Children," *Archives of General Psychiatry* 36, no. 6 (1979): 675, 679.

p. 196 "Several four-year universities . . ." Interviews with representatives of Beacon College, Lynn College, and the University of the Ozarks at the International Meeting of Learning Disabilities Association of America in Chicago, February 2003.

p. 197 "seven intelligences . . ." H. Gardner, *Frames of Mind: The Theory of Multiple Intelligences* (New York: Basic Books, 1983).

p. 197 "gifted and talented programs . . ." M. Levine, "Gifted Children: The Pediatrician's Role," *Pediatric Annals* 14, no. 10 (1985): 693–96.

p. 198 "tells the story of . . ." J. Lerner, Northeast Illinois University, lectures at the Learning Disabilities Association of Texas annual meetings in Austin, 1997–99.

p. 199 "In 1989 . . ." Personal meetings, correspondence, and conversations with Drs. Avrum Katcher and Alfred Healy, 1989.

p. 200 "'inability to regulate inhibition . . .'" R. Barkley, "Shift in Perspective Offers Insights into Biological Nature of ADHD," *AAP News*, April 1999, p. 38.

Bibliography

American Academy of Pediatrics. *Diagnostic and Statistical Manual for Children and Adolescents for Primary Care*. 4th edition. Elk Grove Village, IL: The Academy, 1997.

———. *Toolkit for ADHD*. Elk Grove Village, IL: The Academy, 2002.

American Academy of Pediatrics, Committee on Children with Disabilities. "The American Academy of Pediatrics Defines ADHD." *AAP News*, June 1991, pp. 12–13.

———. "Medication for Children with ADHD." *Pediatrics* 98, no. 6 (1996).

———. "Policy Statement on Newborn Hearing Screening." *Pediatrics* 103, no. 2 (February 1999): 527–30.

———. "The Pediatrician's Role in the Development and Implementation of an IEP and IFSP." *Pediatrics* 104, no. 1 (July 1999).

American Academy of Pediatrics, Committee on Quality Improvement, Subcommittee on ADHD. "Clinical Practice Guidelines: Evaluation of the Child with Attention Deficit/Hyperactivity Disorder." *Pediatrics* 105, no. 5 (May 2000): 1158–70.

———. "Clinical Practice Guideline: Treatment of the School-Aged Child with Attention Deficit/Hyperactivity Disorder." *Pediatrics* 108, no. 4 (October 2001): 1033–44.

Bibliography

American Psychiatric Association. *Diagnostic and Statistical Manual of Mental Disorders.* 2d edition. Washington, D.C.: The Association, 1980.

———. *Diagnostic and Statistical Manual of Mental Disorders.* 3d edition, revised. Washington, D.C.: The Association, 1987.

———. *Diagnostic and Statistical Manual of Mental Disorders.* 4th edition. Washington, D.C.: The Association, 1996.

———. "Practice Parameters for the Use of Stimulant Medications in the Treatment of Children, Adolescents, and Adults." *Journal of the American Academy of Child and Adolescent Psychiatry* 41, supplement 2 (February 2002).

Armstrong, T. *The Myth of the ADD Child: Fifty Ways to Improve Your Child's Behavior and Attention Span without Drugs, Labels, or Coercion.* New York: Dutton, 1995.

Atilla, T., et al., "Long-Term Safety and Efficacy of Respiradone for the Treatment of Disruptive Behavior Disorders in Children with Subaverage I.Q.'s." *Pediatrics* 110, no. 3 (September 2002).

Atkins, D. Lecture at the annual meeting of the American Heart Association. Reported in *Pediatric News*, April 1999, p. 31.

August, G., and B. Garfinkle. "Comorbidity of ADHD and Reading Disability among Clinic-Referred Children." *Journal of Abnormal Child Psychology* 18, no. 1 (February 1990): 29–48.

Baren, M. "Managing ADHD." *Contemporary Pediatrics* 11, no. 12 (December 1994): 29–48.

Barkley, R. "Shift in Perspective Offers Insights into Biological Nature of ADHD." *AAP News*, April 1999, p. 38.

Barkley, R., et al. "Does the Treatment of ADHD with Stimulants Contribute to Drug Use/Abuse? A Thirteen-Year Prospective Study." *Pediatrics* 111, no. 1 (January 2003).

Barkley, R., et al. "Driving-Related Risks and Outcomes in Adolescents and Young Adults: A Three-to-Five Year Follow-Up Survey." *Pediatrics* 92, no. 2 (August 1993): 212–18.

Bibliography

Barkley, R., et al. "Side Effects of Methylphenidate in Children with Attention Deficit Hyperactivity Disorder: A Systematic, Placebo-Controlled Evaluation." *Southern Medical Journal* 83, no. 8 (1990): 947–51.

Barrickman, L., et al. "Bupropion versus Methylphenidate in the Treatment of Attention Deficit Hyperactivity Disorder." *Journal of the American Academy of Child and Adolescent Psychiatry* 34, no. 5 (April 1995): 649–57.

Bates, B. "Medication Makes the Difference in ADHD Children." *Pediatric News* 32, no. 12 (1998): 1.

Batoosingh, K. "Scoping Available Drugs for ADHD Alternatives." *Pediatric News*, March 1995.

Bhutta, A. "Poor Cognitive Outcomes in School-Aged Premies." *Pediatric News*, October 2002.

Biederman, J., et al. "Family Genetic and Psychological Risk Factors in *DSM*-III Attention Deficit Disorder." *Journal of the American Academy of Child and Adolescent Psychiatry* 29, no. 4 (1990): 536–33.

Biederman, J., et al. "Pharmacotherapy of Attention Deficit/Hyperactivity Disorder Reduces Risk for Substance Use Disorder." *Pediatrics* 104, no. 2 (1999): e20.

Biederman, J., et al. "A Randomized Placebo-Controlled Parallel Group Study of Adderall XR in Children with Attention Deficit Hyperactivity Disorder." *Pediatrics* 110, no. 2 (2002): 258–66.

Biederman, J., et al. Data on file. Novartis Pharmaceuticals: Ritalin LA study 002, 007, 97-M-02, Clinical Study and Statistical Report, 2002.

Bradley, C. "The Behavior of Children Receiving Benzedrine." *American Journal of Psychiatry* 94 (1937): 577.

Bradley, C. and M. Bowen. "Amphetamine Therapy of Children's Behavior Disorders." *American Journal of Orthopsychiatry* 11 (1941): 92–103.

Brown, R., and A. Swain. "Cognitive, Neuropsychological, and Academic Sequelae in Children with Leukemia." *Journal of Learning Disabilities* 26, no. 2 (1993): 74–99.

Bibliography

Cantwell, D., and L. Baker. "Association between Attention Deficit Hyperactivity Disorder and Learning Disorders." *Journal of Learning Disabilities* 24, no. 2 (1991): 88–95.

Carter, C., et al., "Effects of a Few-food Diet in Attention Deficit Disorder." *Archives of Diseases in Childhood* 69, no. 5 (1993): 564–68.

Chessells, J. "Treatment of Childhood Lymphoblastic Leukemia: Present Issues and Future Prospects." *Blood Reviews* 6, no. 4 (1992): 193–203.

Chervin, R., et al. "Inattention and Symptoms of Sleep-Disordered Breathing." *Pediatrics* 109, no. 3 (March 2002).

"DataWatch." *Pediatric News* (December 2001): 30.

Ding, Y., et al. "Pharmacokinetics of d and l Methylphenidate in the Human and Baboon Brain." *Psychopharmacology* 131 (1997): 71–78.

Donohue, M. "Low Risk of Death with Tricyclics." *Pediatric News*, April 1999, p. 37.

Duel, R. "Developmental Dysgraphia and Motor Skills Disorders." *Journal of Child Neurology* 1, supplement (1995): 55–59.

Dupree, D. "Pills for Learning." *Wall Street Journal*, January 1971.

Dworkin, P. Lecture before the California Chapter 2 of the American Academy of Pediatrics, Palm Springs, California, March 1999. Reported in *Pediatric News*, April 1999, p. 38.

Feingold, B. *Why Your Child Is Hyperactive*. New York: Random House, 1975.

Franklin, D. "Poor Cognitive Outcomes in School-Aged Preemies." *Pediatric News*, October 2002.

Fungeld, F. "Ginkgo Biloba Extracts." Letter in *The Lancet* 335, no. 8687 (1990): 476.

Gamis, A., and M. Nesbit. "Neuropsychologic Disabilities in Long-Term Survival of Childhood Cancer." *Pediatrician* 18, no. 1 (1991): 11–19.

Gardner, H. *Frames of Mind: The Theory of Multiple Intelligences*. New York: Basic Books, 1983.

Bibliography

Gellis, S. "Report of Liver Failure in a Child on Pemoline." *Pediatric Notes*, no. 6 (1998).

Glacola, G. "Cocaine in the Cradle: A Hidden Epidemic." *Southern Medical Journal* 83, no. 8 (1990): 947–51.

Goodman, L., et al., "Diagnosis and Treatment of Attention Deficit Disorder in Children and Adolescents." *JAMA* 279, no. 14 (1998): 1100–107.

Goodman, R., and J. Stevenson. "A Twin Study of Hyperactivity: The Aetilogical Role of Genes, Family Relationships, and Perinatal Adversity." *Journal of Child Psychology and Psychiatry* 30, no. 5 (1989): 691–709.

Gooze, A., and E. Gooze. *Operating Instructions for the Differently Wired Child.* Austin, TX: Communications and Learning Services, 1999.

Greenhill, L., et al. "A Double-Blind Placebo Study of Modified-Release Methylphenidate in Children with Attention Deficit Hyperactivity Disorder." *Pediatrics* 109, no. 3 (March 2002): e39.

Greenhill, L., et al., and the American Psychiatric Association. "Practice Parameters for the Use of Stimulant Medications in the Treatment of Children, Adolescents, and Adults." *Journal of the American Academy of Child and Adolescent Psychiatry* 41, supplement 2 (February 2002).

Haber, J., and the Texas Pediatric Society Committee on Children with Disabilities. *How Do I Get Help for My Child with a School Problem?* Rev. ed. Austin: Texas Pediatric Society, 2002.

Halpern, D. "Scientists Pinpoint Dosage of Melatonin for Insomnia." MIT Tech Talk. Massachusetts Institute of Technology, October 2001.

Halsam, R. "Is There a Role for Megavitamin Therapy in the Treatment of Attention Deficit Hyperactivity Disorders?" *Advances in Neurology* 58 (1992): 303–10.

Halterman, J., et al. "Iron Deficiency Anemia and Cognitive Achievement Among School-Age Children and Adolescents in the United States." *Pediatrics* 107, no. 6 (June 2001).

Bibliography

Harley, J. "Synthetic Food Colors and Hyperactivity in Children: A Double-Blind Challenge Experiment." *Pediatrics* 62 (1978): 975.

Hart, C. "Fifty Percent of Fragile X Patients Lack Telltale Signs." *AAP News* 14, no. 6 (1999): 1, 16.

Hauser, P., et al. "Attention Deficit Hyperactivity Disorder in People with Generalized Resistant Thyroid Hormone." *The New England Journal of Medicine* 328, no. 14 (1993): 997–1001.

Hazell, P., et al. "Diagnosis and Treatment of ADHD Plague Australia Too." *Medical Journal of Australia* 165, no. 9 (1996): 477–80.

Healy, A., J. Haber, and A. Katcher. "The AAP Committee on Children with Disabilities Defines Attention Deficit Hyperactivity Disorder." *AAP News* 7, no. 8 (1991): 12–13.

Hentoff, N. "The Drugged Classroom." *Evergreen Review* 14 (1970): 31.

Hughes, C., et al. "Cognitive Performance at School Age of Very Low Birth Weight Infants with Bronchopulmonary Dysplasia." *Journal of Developmental and Behavioral Pediatrics* 20, no. 1 (1999): 1–8.

Hunt, R., et al. "Clonidine Benefits Children with ADD and Hyperactivity: Report of a Double-Blind Study Placebo-Crossover Therapeutic Trial." *Journal of the American Academy of Child and Adolescent Psychiatry* 24, no. 5 (1985): 617–29.

Hynd, G., et al. "Attention Deficit Disorder without Hyperactivity: A Distinct Behavioral and Neurocognitive Syndrome." *Journal of Child Neurology* 6 (1991): 37–43.

Hynd, G., et al. "Brain Morphology in Developmental Dyslexia and ADHD." *Archives of Neurology* 47, no. 8 (1990): 919–26.

Hynd, G., et al. "Corpus Callosum Morphology in Attention Deficit Hyperactivity Disorder Morphometric Analysis of MRI." *Journal of Learning Disabilities* 24, no. 3 (1991): 141–46.

Irlene, H. *Reading by the Colors*. New York: Avenbury Press, 1991.

Johnson, D., "Toolkit for ADHD." *AAP News*, August 2000.

Bibliography

Kass, C. "Final Report U.S.O.E. Contract for Advanced Institute for Leadership Personnel in Learning Disabilities." Washington, D.C.: U.S. Department of Education, 1970.

Kass, C., and H. Myklebust. "Learning Disability: An Educational Definition." *Journal of Learning Disabilities* 2 (1969): 38–40.

Kauffman, J., and D. Hallahan. *The Illusion of Full Inclusion: A Comprehensive Critique of a Current Special Education Bandwagon.* Austin, TX: Pro-Ed, 1995.

Kelly, D., and G. Aylward. "Attention Deficit in School-Aged Children and Adolescents: Current Issues and Practices." *Pediatric Clinics of North America* 39, no. 3 (1992): 487–512.

Kelly, D., et al. "Attention Deficit in Children and Adolescents with Hearing Loss: A Survey." *American Journal of Diseases of Children* 147, no. 7 (1993): 737–41.

Korman, R. "Cognitive Event–Related Potentials in Attention Deficit Disorder." *Journal of Learning Disabilities* 24, no. 3 (1991): 130–40.

Kosofsky, B. "Cocaine-Induced Alterations in Neurodevelopment." *Seminars in Speech and Language* 19, no. 2 (1998): 109–21.

Landman, G. "Alternative Therapies." In *Developmental-Behavioral Pediatrics*, 2d. edition, edited by M. Levine, W. Carey, and A. Crocker. Philadelphia: Saunders, 1992.

Levine, E., and B. Burke. "ADHD in Coastal Virginia." *Social Work Today*, July 8, 2002.

Levine, M. "Attention Variation and Dysfunction." In *Developmental-Behavioral Pediatrics*, 2d. edition, edited by M. Levine, W. Carey, and A. Crocker. Philadelphia: Saunders, 1992.

———. "Gifted Children: The Pediatrician's Role." *Pediatric Annals* 14, no. 10 (1985): 693–96.

Levy, F. "A Study of Twins in Australia: Genetics Plays an Important Role in ADHD Comorbidity." Presentation at the annual meeting of the American Academy of Child and Adolescent Psychology. Reported in *Pediatric News*, February 1998, p. 30.

Bibliography

Lindamood, P., et al. "Sensory-Cognitive Factors in the Controversy over Reading Instruction." *Journal of Developmental and Learning Disorders* 1, no. 1 (1997).

Linde, K., et al. "Saint-John's-Wort for Depression: An Overview and Meta-analysis of Randomized Clinical Trials." *British Medical Journal* 313, no. 7052 (1996): 253–58.

Lubar, J. "Discourse on the Development of EEG Diagnostics and Biofeedback for Attention Deficit Hyperactivity Disorders." *Biofeedback and Self-Regulation* 16, no. 3 (1991): 201–25.

———. "Neocortical Dynamics: Implication for Understanding the Role of Neurofeedback and Related Techniques for Enhancement of Attention." *Applied Psychophysiology of Biofeedback* 22, no. 2 (1997): 111–26.

Lubar, J., et al. "Evaluation of the Effectiveness of EEG Neurofeedback Training for ADHD in a Clinical Setting as Measured by TOVA Scores, Behavior Ratings, and WISC-R Performance." *Biofeedback and Self-Regulation* 20, no. 1 (1995): 83–95.

Mann, C., et al. "Quantatitive Analysis of EEG in Boys with ADHD: Controlled Study with Clinical Implications." *Pediatric Neurology* 8, no. 1 (1992): 30–36.

Mannuzza, S., et al. "Hyperactive Boys Almost Grown Up; V. Replication of Psychiatric Status." *Archives of General Psychiatry* 48 (1991): 77–78.

Maynard, R. "Omaha Students Given Behavior Drugs." *Washington Post*, June 29, 1970.

McCarney, S. *Attention Deficit Disorder Evaluation Scale, School Version.* 2d edition. Columbia, MO: Hawthorne Education Services, 1995.

Michaelson, D., et al. "Atomoxetine in the Treatment of Children and Adolescents with Attention-Deficit/Hyperactivity Disorder: A Randomized, Placebo-Controlled, Dose-Response Study" *Pediatrics* 108, no. 5 (2001): e83.

Bibliography

Mick, E., et al. "Import of Low Birth Weight on Attention-Deficit Hyperactivity Disorder." *Journal of Developmental and Behavioral Pediatrics* 23, no. 1 (February 2002): 16–22.

Modi, N. and B. Lindermuler. "Single and Multiple Dose Pharmacokinetics of an Oral Once-a-Day, Osmotic, Controlled Release OROS (Methylphenidate) Formulation." *Journal of Clinical Pharmacology* 40 (2000): 379–88.

MTA Cooperative Group. "A Fourteen-Month Randomized Clinical Trial of Treatment Strategies for ADHD: Multimodal Treatment Study of Children with ADHD." *Archives of General Psychiatry* 56, no. 12 (1999): 1073–86.

Munte, T., et al. "Effects of Kava Roots on Event-Related Potentials in a Word Recognition Task." *Neuropsychobiology* 27, no. 1 (1993): 46–53.

Needleman, H., et al. "The Long-Term Effects to Low Doses of Lead in Childhood: An Eleven-Year Follow-up Report." *The New England Journal of Medicine* 322, no. 2 (1990): 83–85.

Norris, C. "Special Tips for Parents." In *How Do I Get Help For My Child with a School Problem?* Fort Worth Child Study Center version. Austin: Texas Pediatric Society, 2003.

Oski, F., ed. *Principles and Practice of Pediatrics.* 2d edition. Philadelphia: Lippincott, 1994.

Pelham, W., and H. Aronoff. "A Comparison of Ritalin and Adderall: Efficacy and Time Course in Children with ADHD." *Pediatrics* 103, no. 4 (1999): e43.

Pelham, W., et al. "Sustained Release and Standard Methylphenidate Effects on Cognitive and Social Behavior in Children with ADD." *Pediatrics* 80, no. 4 (1987): 491–501.

Perlman, J. "Neurobehavioral Deficits in Premature Graduates of Intensive Care: Potential Medical and Neonatal Environmental Risk Factors." *Pediatrics* 108, no. 6 (December 2001).

Phelps, J. et al. *Children's Handwriting Evaluation Scale: A New Diagnostic Tool.* Dallas: Dallas Scottish Rite Hospital, 1984.

Bibliography

Physician's Desk Reference. Montvale, NJ: Medical Economics Press, 2002.

Physician's Desk Reference for Herbal Medicines. Montvale, NJ: Medical Economics Press, 1999.

Pliska, S. "Tricyclic Antidepressants in the Treatment of Children with an ADHD Disorder." *Journal of the American Academy of Child and Adolescent Psychiatry* 26, no. 2 (1987): 127–33.

Putman, G. "How to Get the Best from Your ADD Colleagues." *Advances for Occupational Therapy Practitioners,* February 16, 1998.

Rapp, D. *Is This Your Child? Discovering and Treating Unrecognized Allergies in Children and Adults.* New York: Quill/W. Morrow, 1991.

Robinson, N. "Educational Options for Gifted Children." *Pediatric Annals* 14, no. 10 (1985): 745–50.

Rogers, G. Lecture. Annual meeting of the American Academy of Pediatrics. San Francisco: October 1998.

Rogers, J. "Drug Abuse—Just What the Doctor Ordered." *Psychology Today* 16 (1971): 20.

Ruze, P. "Kava-Induced Dermopathy: A Niacin Deficiency?" *The Lancet* 335, no. 8703 (1990): 1442–45.

Safer, D., et al. "Increased Methylphenidate Usage for Attention Deficit Hyperactivity Disorder in the 1990's." *Pediatric* 98, no. 1 (1996): 1084–88.

Saigol, S. "Meeting on Developmental Disabilities, Johns Hopkins University, March 1999." *Pediatric News,* June 1999, p. 12.

Senf, G. "Learning Disabilities." *Pediatric Clinics of North America* 20, no. 2 (1973): 607–40.

Shaywitz, S., and B. Shaywitz. "Diagnosis and Management of Attention Deficit Disorder: A Pediatric Perspective." *Pediatric Clinics of North America* 31, no. 2 (1984): 429–57.

Singer, L., et al. "Childhood Medical and Behavioral Consequences of Maternal Cocaine Use." *Journal of Pediatric Psychology* 17, no. 4 (1992): 389–406.

Skertic, M. *Chicago Sun-Times,* winter 2002. Article series.

Bibliography

Société Canadienne de pédiatrie. "Megavitamin and Mineral Therapy in Childhood." *Canadian Medical Association Journal* 143, no. 10 (1990): 1009–13.

Sommerfelt, K. "Long-Term Outcome for Non-Handicapped Low Birth Weight Infants: Is the Fog Clearing?" *European Journal of Pediatrics* 57, no. 1 (1998): 1–3.

Speer, F. "The Allergic Tension Fatigue Syndrome." *Pediatric Clinics of North America* 1 (1954): 1029.

Spenser, T., et al. "ADHD and Thyroid Abnormalities: A Research Note." *Journal of Child Psychiatry* 36, no. 5 (1995): 879–85.

Sprague, R., and E. Sleator. "Effects of Psychopharmacological Agents on Learning Disorders." *Pediatric Clinics of North America* 20, no. 3 (1973): 720.

Stein, M., and J. Perrin. "Diagnosis and Evaluation of Children with ADHD." *Pediatrics* 105, no. 5 (May 2000).

Stockbridge, L. U.S. Food and Drug Administration, Division of Drug Marketing, Advertising, and Communication. Letter. November 2000.

Strauss, A., et al. *Psychopathology and Education of the Brain-Injured Child.* 2 vols. New York: Grune and Stratton, 1947–1955.

Sullivan, M. "Stimulants Given Despite Evidence of an ADHD Diagnosis." *Pediatric News*, August 2002.

Swanson, J., et al. "Initiating Concerta (OROS) Methylphenidate in Children with Attention Deficit Hyperactivity Disorder." *Journal of Clinical Research* 3 (October 2000): 59–76.

Thompson, T. "Risk of Adolescent Pregnancy in the United States." *Department of Human Health Services/Centers for Disease Control Bulletin*, November 2002.

Trope, I., et al. "Effects of Lead on Brain Metabolism." *Pediatrics* 107, no. 6 (2001): 1437–43.

Tyler, V. *Herbs of Choice: The Therapeutic Use of Phytomedicinals.* New York: Pharmaceutical Products Press, 1994.

Bibliography

———. *The Honest Herbal: A Sensible Guide to the Use of Herbs and Related Remedies.* 3d edition. New York: Pharmaceutical Products Press, 1993.

Ulman, R., and E. Sleator. "Responders, Nonresponders, and Placebo Responders among Children with Attention Deficit Disorder: Importance of a Blinded Placebo Evaluation." *Clinical Pediatrics* 25, no. 12 (1986): 594–99.

United States Drug Enforcement Administration. Yearly aggregate production quotas. Washington, D.C.: Drug Enforcement Administration Department of Public Affairs, 1995.

Volkow, N., et al. "Dopamine Transporter Occupancies in the Human Brain Induced by Therapeutic Doses of Oral Methylphenidate." *American Journal of Psychiatry* 155, no. 10 (1998): 1325–31.

Weinberg, W., and R. Brumback. "The Myth of Attention Deficit Hyperactivity Disorder: Symptoms Resulting from Multiple Causes." *Journal of Child Neurology* no. 10, supplement (1995).

———. "Hyperactivity in Childhood." *The New England Journal of Medicine* 323, no. 20 (1990): 675–81.

Weiss, G. and L. Hechtman "Hyperactives as Young Adults: A Controlled Prospective Ten-Year Follow-up Study of Seventy-five Children." *Archives of General Psychiatry* 36, no. 6 (1979): 675–81.

Whitaker, A., et al. "Psychiatric Outcomes in Low-Birth-Weight Children at Age Six Years: Relation to Neonatal Cranial Ultrasound Abnormalities." *Archives of General Psychiatry* 54, no. 9 (1997): 847–56.

Whitfield, M., et al. "Extremely Premature School Children: Multiple Areas of Hidden Disability." *Archives of Diseases in Childhood* 77, no. 2 (1997): F85–F90.

Wilkins, A., et al. "Transplacental Cocaine Exposure: Effects of Cocaine Dose and Gestational Timing." *Neurotoxicology Teratology* 20, no. 3 (1998): 227–38.

Bibliography

Wolraich, M., et al. "Stimulant Medication Use by Primary Care Physicians in the Treatment of ADHD." *Pediatrics* 86, no. 1 (1990): 95–101.

Wong, A., et al. "Herbal Remedies in Psychiatric Practice." *Archives of General Psychiatry* 55, no. 11 (1998): 1033–44.

World Almanac and Book of Facts. New York: World Almanac Books, 1998.

Zametkin, A., et al. "Cerebral Glucose Metabolism in Adults with Hyperactivity of Childhood Onset." *The New England Journal of Medicine* 323, no. 20 (1990): 1361–66.

Zito, M., et al. "Trends in Prescribing Psychotropic Medication to Preschoolers." *JAMA* 283, no. 8 (February 23, 2000).

Index

Index